In the Shadow of Cooks

In the Shadow of Cooks

✦

How Come the Chicken Isn't Getting Brown

Training the Next Wave of Culinary Professionals

A book by Paul Sorgule, CCE, AAC

iUniverse, Inc.
New York Lincoln Shanghai

In the Shadow of Cooks
How Come the Chicken Isn't Getting Brown

iUniverse books may be ordered through booksellers or by contacting:

iUniverse
2021 Pine Lake Road, Suite 100
Lincoln, NE 68512
www.iuniverse.com
1-800-Authors (1-800-288-4677)

The views expressed in this work are solely those of the author and do not necessarily reflect the views of the publisher, and the publisher hereby disclaims any responsibility for them.

ISBN: 978-0-595-43695-8 (pbk)
ISBN: 978-0-595-88029-4 (ebk)

Printed in the United States of America

This book is dedicated to the most important people in my life: my wife Sharon, my children—Erika, Jessica and Leif; my mother Katherine and my father Earl, Gene and Joan Pembroke; my friends—Rick and Janice Zloty, Cheryl Ploof, Tracey Caponera, Jim and Jo Bestine, Doug Appleton, Bob and Lori Appleton, Kenneth and Noelle Weissberg, Audrey and Christopher Weissberg, Curtiss and Bridget Hemm, Charles and Torill Carroll, Mickey and Kathy Beriau, George and Wendy Higgins, Anton and Pam Flory, Noble and Robin Masi, Joe Faria, Lars and Ingrid Johansson, Steve Schimoler and Robin Schempp, Kim and Wendy, Neil and Kathy Connolly, Joel and Karen Dekkers, Jake and "D" Jacobs, Ed and Lisa Weibrecht, Mary Peterson, Walter and Phoebe Zuromski, Jamie Keating, Eamon Lee, Dave and Dan Russ, John and Debbie McBride, Don Benjamin, Ron Butler, Pat and Phillip Flath, Fran and George Peroni, Tim Sullivan, Christine McCoy, David and Lynn Johnson, Tom and Betsy Minehan, Greg Michaud, Jason Porter, Tim McQuinn, Katie Welch, my entire crew at the Mirror Lake Inn, and the chefs and students with whom I have been associated over the years.

Special thanks to Professor Robert (Bo Jest) Seidenstein for his skills at copy editing this book.

Contents

Introduction

A baby is born. It cries, it is fed, it is content. From our first moments of life we have a close bond with food. Is our first feeling of contentment love for our mother or love for the food that she brings us?

Certainly we grow up to love our mother for who she is and how she cares for us, but in the beginning, how powerful is that connection to food? Throughout our lives, from that first moment on, there is a connection, of varying degrees, between the psychological and physiological gratification that food provides. It fills our stomachs when we are hungry, warms our body when we are cold, quenches our thirst when our bodies crave hydration, enhances our times of celebration, consummates our feelings of self-worth, repairs damages to bruised egos, comforts us when we are sad, calms us when we are mad, and strokes us when we need a boost.

Food can be addictive, it can become an aphrodisiac, it can inspire creative thought, it can represent artistic genius, it can make us remember, it can make us forget. Food is the universal language, the one thing that can bind people of different beliefs and backgrounds and can even bridge the gaps that culture tends to create.

Throughout a person's life, every contact that is made is somehow stored in their subconscious. The impact of each contact varies, but some continue to influence the direction and outcomes that become a person's life experience, forever.

This is a story of a network of common people from average backgrounds who shared a passion for food since their birth and who sought opportunities to aspire to greatness through involvement with cooking and the crazy people who call the kitchen their home. Their impact on me (the story's main character) continues to this very moment.

It takes a lot of nerve to write a story about parts of your own life and assume that anyone would have even a fleeting interest in the content, but that is exactly what I did. Why? Who knows? I guess it is just one of those things a person feels compelled to do. Maybe it is because too many people have felt a cook is a cook and could never be considered anything else. Maybe it is just one of those things you want to check off your list after the age of 50.

I have left out a great deal to protect the innocent and my own personal reputation. Everyone I know who reads this can fill in the blanks and keep those details to themselves. The foundations are here and that is all that I care to expose. Some of the characters in this book are fictitious, but all are based upon an understanding of people and their innate promise of greatness, as witnessed through my own experiences.

If anyone is looking for inspiration in these words, good luck. It was not written with that intent. It simply is what it is: a book about a cook, a chef, a teacher and his friends.

1

Interesting characters

Steve was born in Binghamton, New York, home to Endicott Johnson Shoes and typical as an "Upstate New York" (anything north of New York City) town. Neighborhoods were close, schools were filled with friends from next door, and families worked in the community and spent what little money they had in local businesses.

Steve grew up like any other small-town kid, not giving too much thought to his future until junior year in high school. His family rarely traveled, only went out to restaurants for special occasions and even then the food of choice was some form of ground meat, steak, or freezer-to-fryer special. Steve's exposure to the hospitality industry was limited.

As a student, Steve was truly "average." At least his commitment to his high school classes was average. He did what he had to, found no real usefulness to the topics presented, knew he had to graduate, but had no real aspirations or goals beyond that.

During the summer between his sophomore and junior year, Steve obtained his first job as a dishwasher in the local Holiday Inn. The property was relatively small with 200 guest rooms, three banquet rooms of varying size, and a full-service restaurant that was open for breakfast, lunch and dinner.

Steve took an instant liking to the environment. People were up-front, in your face, everyday, "real" individuals who were never afraid to speak their minds, and were generally hard working and full of interesting stories. Little did Steve realize that this first job experience would set the stage for the rest of his life.

Sabine was not the most popular girl in high school. She was shy, fairly short compared to her peers, not terribly interested in anything but sports, and only average as a student. Her hometown of Wheeling, Illinois was regarded only as a suburb of Chicago. However, unlike Steve's neighborhood where people were fairly close, if you wanted to make a respectable living, you would probably commute to Chicago rather than seek employment in Wheeling.

Sabine played baseball, ran relay on the high school track team, played competitive hockey during the winter months, and knew every NFL player, on every team, along with their important statistics. Sports were what she did. Playing and watching sports were the only serious things on her mind, period.

In 1986 she took her first job at a well-known restaurant in Wheeling as a vegetable prep cook. Little did she realize that this particular restaurant would become the number-one French restaurant in the United States. To her the job complemented her love for physical activity. The work was hard, people were serious about their work, the pace was fast, and every day the staff was focused on a goal.

True, she was the only female employee in the kitchen, but despite warnings from others, she did not find any bias or testosterone-laced banter taking place in the kitchen that was hurtful or demeaning. In fact, once she proved herself as a dependable, hard-worker with a desire to learn, she was treated with the same respect everyone else was afforded.

Jerome grew up in a family of privilege. They were not wealthy, but the nature of his parents' work allowed the family to travel quite a bit. Jerome had been to Europe three times by the time he was twelve and by the time he began his sophomore year in high school he had visited 22 of the United States.

Jerome knew how to assess quality hotels and restaurants. His educated palate was very prepared to accept everything from foie gras to truffles and free-range chicken to Kobe Beef. His family taught him how to dress as a young professional, exposed him to fine music and art, and built in Jerome an appreciation for proper etiquette.

Although he had never worked in a professional kitchen, he did cook at home. While many of his classmates were shooting hoops after school, Jerome was walking through the markets of Dean and DeLucca on Prince and Broadway looking for ingredients to experiment with at home.

New York City was more than his home. It was his inspiration. He always admired the people, the pace of the city, the style, the culture, and of course the affluence of its inhabitants.

During the summer between his junior and senior year, Jerome took a position as a bus boy at Veritas in downtown Manhattan. Jerome was able to dress professionally and mingle with New York's hip young careerists while he set tables, polished silver, folded napkins, poured bottled water and transferred artisan rolls and breads from warming baskets to bread and butter plates. Occasionally, the chef would let him try some of the incredible creations from the kitchen of Veritas and even taste a few of the wines from their extraordinary cellars.

His culture of privilege led him to believe that some day, he too would own a respectable restaurant like Veritas. His desire was to feed his passion for food by learning as much as he could, but then spend his time mingling with guests, promoting the restaurant and building its image.

Meredith knew she wanted to be an artist from the first time she took a class in watercolors during the summer of 1982. Next year she would be in high school and already she was convinced that her future career would evolve around fine art.

Growing up in Rutland, Vermont, Meredith learned to love nature and the Green Mountains, where she would hike with her parents and friends. When she painted, it was almost always a picture of mountains, streams and trees. Her mother raised six children and still managed to operate an "at home" cake decorating business. Typically, five or six wedding cakes and dozens of birthday and other special occasion cakes left their kitchen every month. By the time Meredith entered high school, her mother and father had converted their garage into a professional bakery.

Meredith quickly learned how to handle a pastry bag and how to produce picture-perfect roses and cake borders. Business was so good that her parents put her on the payroll part-time during the school year and full-time in the summer. There was no need for Meredith to find another job, the family business was *it*. Ironically, her desire to be an artist was satisfied in this bakery environment and in fact many of her creations used the nature she loved as inspiration.

Meredith also learned that the business came first. Many family events were put on hold when business dictated a need for yet another cake, or two, or ten. She became accustomed to holidays falling on a different day than everyone else's. This, of course, would become an important piece of knowledge in her future.

Graham lived in Rochester, New York. Home to Kodak and Xerox, it was considered a right of passage for many to complete their education and work for one of these two companies. This would not be the case with Graham.

From early on, it was apparent to everyone who knew him, that Jerome loved competition. If he played chess, he wanted to learn how to win; if he played touch football, he played with the intensity of a professional; when rode bikes with his friends, every trip became the Tour de France.

Graham was a latch key kid during his final years in middle school. Both his parents worked and told Graham to come home directly after school, set the dinner table, and in some cases, put dinner in the oven. Long before the Food Network would emerge as a channel in its own right, Graham found and became fascinated with shows like Julia Child and the Galloping Gourmet. He started to experiment with the meals based on what he observed on these shows, and received rave reviews from his parents.

When he turned sixteen, he started working part-time at the Marriott Hotel. He worked in the banquet kitchen with a chef who not only had an extensive background in food preparation; he was also a competition chef. Graham had not realized that there were forums for chefs to compete. His interest in everything else ceased. He now had a clear idea how he would focus his future career.

Finally, Jacob was an Army brat. His father was a master sergeant with the United States Army. Over Jacob's first 13 years on this planet, he had lived on four different Army bases. Although he was around people his own age, most of his friends were the soldiers his father worked with. His father's rank gave Jacob a few special privileges. He had free reign of most areas on a post and often gravitated to the mess hall. He liked the people here and always had an opportunity to eat. Army cooks liked Jacob and usually tossed him an apron and put him to work peeling vegetables and of course, washing pots and pans.

When the military decided to privatize much of the work done in military base kitchens, Jacob applied for a job. In 1984, with working papers in hand, Jacob was on the road to a career in quantity food service.

Coming from different backgrounds, but with food as a common denominator, all of these future professionals found their way to the halls of culinary education and at some point, in my classroom. This is a story about the trials and tribulations of teaching, the pains and joys of working in kitchens, and the fulfillment of young people's dreams.

In the beginning there was food.

It was 1950, America was free of war (temporarily), Levittown style housing complexes were cropping up all over the country and a new definition of community was being born. The "block" was suddenly being defined as a cluster of young families, all in their first homes, having kids and creating that "leave it to Beaver" environment that seemed to fit the American Dream.

I was an average, albeit shorter than the norm, young boy growing up in Buffalo, New York. My dreams were simple: get home from school as soon as possible, change clothes and play with the kids on the block. That was it. No greater vision, no smaller needs, just being accepted and having an opportunity to discover fun.

Through all the trials and tribulations of growing up, going to school, the occasional joke about my height, the moderate pressures to perform in school at a level that would prepare me for college, I remained content to live life as I had for the past 15 years, only seeking acceptance from my peers and a chance to have fun.

Sixteen is a tough year. First jobs, junior year in high school, standardized tests demonstrating potential for success in college, and—God forbid—the thought of choosing a career. What does the typical sixteen-year old male want to do? How about becoming a rock star, or maybe a racecar driver? Practical choices wouldn't make sense for a sixteen year old.

The pressures placed on young people to choose can either be overwhelming or comical. Make a choice! Do something that makes sense! Time is running out! So what do you do? When all else fails, the average student of life reflects back on his or her vast experiences for real wisdom.

My first job was in a kitchen—washing dishes, of course. The pearl diver, dish scum, king of the sinks, commanding general of the garbage disposal, friend of every cat in the neighborhood and brunt of everyone's moods in the kitchen. The only saving grace is that the job is mindless and at the end of the week you get that beloved paycheck. Minimum wage is not much, but to a sixteen year-old it was my own cash, nobody else's, no more begging for an allowance, my money.

Kitchen people were interesting. They were often crude, which to a sixteen-year-old boy was pretty cool. The jokes were raw, but definitely funny. Observations of people, employees and customers were well focused and right on track with even the most sophisticated psychological analysis. The best part was the ability to eat what you wanted, when you wanted, and as much as you wanted. Not a bad job after all.

Millie was the short-order cook. As caring as a mother, as rough as a truck driver, as honest as a priest, as organized as a NASA engineer, and as competent a craftsman as any sculptor or painter, this was Millie.

Millie's husband had been a *"chef."* As she pointed out to me, chefs were different from short-order cooks. They were somehow elevated to a level of prestige, at least in Millie's mind, which should cause anyone to stop and take notice of whatever they do or say. Her husband, unfortunately, had passed away and left Millie with her grown children and a second-string desire to keep the passion alive through the hands of short-order cooking.

Now, it is important to understand that a short-order cook, a good one, is masterful at what they do. They are competent technicians and "real-life" entertainers. Millie was such a craftsman. "Three orders of eggs over easy, two flap jacks, three rashers of bacon, an egg in a basket, and western omelette. Pick-up on table five, the party of four shirred eggs and the two waffle orders for table seven. By the way, Joe wants to know if he can get two fried egg sandwiches on hard rolls to go right away, he has to get back to work in ten minutes." From six-thirty a.m. until lunch ended at two, this was the minute-by-minute dialogue that took place between the waitresses (back then you never saw waiters in restaurants of this type) and the cook. The cook ruled with an iron frying pan. It would be decades before any restaurant started to believe that the customer was ever right. If Millie said no, that was the end of the story.

I was fascinated by the organization, the symmetry of motion, the speed of the process, the unique language that servers and cooks had developed (BLT for Bacon, Lettuce and Tomato sandwich; Two Looking At You for eggs cooked sunny side up; Wreck Them for scrambled eggs; Black and Blue for a steak seared on the outside and raw on the inside), and the sheer power that Millie exuded. It didn't take long before I asked Millie if I could occasionally shed my role as master pearl diver and join her on the short-order platform of glory.

Millie was impressed with my interest and took me under her wing. Before long, I was grilling danish for those early-to-rise construction workers, scrambling eggs, making Joe his fried egg sandwiches, helping the waitresses make coffee (it was hard not to have a crush on those college girls who waitressed in the summer months), cleaning grills, cutting French fries, shaping hamburg patties, and prepping garnishes for the stampede of hungry patrons who walked through the doors from six-thirty a.m. till two. By the end of that first summer in a kitchen, I had risen to the ranks of "assistant" short-order cook.

Now, it was probably fate that I would begin my working life in a kitchen. My grandfather, great uncle, great aunt and grandmother all either worked in or owned restaurants and taverns.

My early memories of dining out were not that extraordinary. The weekly fish fry was either take-out or sit down at a traditional restaurant with average food and a very attentive waitress who knew the entire family by first name. Fast food was just in its infancy, and most restaurant experiences were still reserved for "special occasions." The diner style operation that I worked in was true Americana. An offshoot of the "Greek Diner" that sprouted up at every major intersection in the United States it was really a tribute to locals looking for the opportunity to share a story and a cup of coffee, or to those transients stopping to refresh and fill up their cars with gas.

By the end of August, on the verge of my sixteenth birthday, I had decided on a career in the hotel/restaurant trade. Mom and Dad, of course, were pleased that talk of being a rock star was now on the proverbial back burner, but subtle pressure was placed on me to focus on the "management" of these areas rather than continuing thoughts of becoming a cook. I didn't care; at least I had an answer when people asked, "So what are you going to do after high school?"

The college trips were not as painful as I had imagined. My grades in high school were acceptable, but nothing to write home about. Obviously, Harvard and Yale would not be on my list. In researching schools for Hotel and Restaurant Management, the process was rather quick, since only a few existed in 1967. A trip to three yielded a simple answer. "I want to go to the one that is furthest away." Actually, that was not the answer verbalized, even though most high school seniors were anxious to find schools where they could "find themselves" and express their independence. Being close to home would certainly cramp one's style.

A school in the Adirondacks of New York seemed perfect. Seven hours away, in the middle of nowhere, a campus that resembled Boy Scout camp, plenty of bars in close proximity, and the degree program that I was looking for. I made the choice, Paul Smith's College (where the hell is Paul Smith's?).

I was able to convince my best friend, Rick, that college was in his best interest as well, and that going to Paul Smith's would be an interesting way to prepare for a career and enjoy the pleasures of independence at the same time. We both packed our bags and left for the Adirondacks.

By the way, the person most pleased about my choice was Millie, the short-order goddess. When I left my summer job for the college quest, Millie gave me the set of cookbooks that her husband, the chef, had cherished during his career. A gift that would never be forgotten, this was to be a divine sign that would later point me in the right direction.

College was great! Grades aside, I learned a great deal about people, kitchen people in particular, snow, driving in snow, a more than cursory exposure to the joys and sorrows of consuming alcohol and the like, and ahh … that feeling of independence. Of course, there is usually a thing or two that gets in the way of the finer things in life. In 1968, that was Vietnam.

All through high school there were occasional discussions about the war in some obscure part of the world, and quite a few friends from school actually dropped out to join the Army or Marines and enjoy the pleasures of seeing the world, compliments of Uncle Sam. Unfortunately, some of those accidental tourists never came home again. It was the later part of 1969 when reality struck. The first U.S. draft lottery would define who would be drawn into this conflict as unwilling recruits and who would avoid the hook of Sergeant Bilko. Hardly fair, but as they say, all is fair in love and war.

Sitting in front of the television with a cluster of seventeen-year-old male students, I did not need to wait very long. December 29 was the 17th draw in the lottery. I was certainly within the reach of Uncle Sam, and the days of wine and roses were probably coming to an end.

Fortunately, an opening in the National Guard circumvented the call to arms that would have followed my "pass with flying colors" draft physical results. Six years as a part-time warrior on U.S. soil would certainly be preferred to a one year tour of duty in Vietnam, where some of my high school acquaintances visited and never returned from. Enough mellow-drama.

The Real-World

The National Guard wasn't bad. Basic training with the Army, two weeks of training every year, and one weekend a month for six years seemed like a reasonable alternative. While I waited for my basic training orders, I took a job as a "manager" of a pizza crust commissary. Not bad! Two years of college, a few courses shy of a degree, 19 years old and already a manager.

The Dilbert Principle is derived from a belief that all managers are idiots. In my case, this was absolutely true. I had as much business being a manager as I would a brain surgeon. Managers need to know something about people. I knew very little. Managers need to know something about production systems. I knew very little. Managers need to know something about the finances of a business. This was not my forte in college.

Try on a typical day at the pizza commissary with me in charge

King's Pizza was a small chain of restaurants. They all shared a common menu, but lacked consistency in product. The owner, a marginally educated, naive business person, decided that building a commissary to pre-make and partially bake crusts was the best way to go. So he bought a fairly sophisticated system that included huge 300 pound dough mixers, conveyor dough cutters and molders, automated conveyor proof boxes for dough, press machines that would shape the proofed dough to fit a pizza pan and massive ferris wheel ovens that could accommodate 42 pizza crusts at a time, with an average partial bake time of four minutes. Crusts would cool in mobile racks, be bagged in packages of six, cool under refrigeration overnight and be delivered the next morning to his six pizza shops in the Buffalo area.

After interviewing numerous candidates for the position of "manager," I was the shining star. After all, I went to college for restaurant management. Of course, I knew absolutely nothing about pizza crust, baking, production systems, training employees, helping employees to self-motivate, scheduling, etc.

After two weeks of pizza training at one of the King's restaurants, I was moved to the new commissary and instructed in the fine art of running a food plant. Four employees were hired, I was given the keys to the insane asylum and the owner basically said, "good luck."

Day one was trial and error—actually, more error than trial. Getting the dough formula just right was challenging enough, but getting the timing of mixing, bowl proof, cutting and shaping, proof time, pressing and oven consistency were mind-boggling.

I may have produced a few dozen "usable" crusts that day. Fine, practice makes perfect. Oh, by the way, why is this damn place so hot? By the end of that first disastrous day, everyone was soaking wet, the place looked like a bomb went off, and there was very little to show for our collective effort.

A profile of the employees would be in order. John was a seventeen-year old high school drop out. A nice kid, but he lacked any real life focus. Mark was very strange. He had more tattoos than fingers and toes, never said a word, and smelled like the bar down the street. Jimmy had worked in restaurants before and actually had spent the last two years running one of King's Pizza Shops. For some reason he thought that the commissary manager's job should have been his. Finally, there was Jake, who was somehow connected to the owner of King's. He wasn't a relative, but probably the son of a friend, of a friend. He had the distinct privilege of living in an apartment over the commissary.

Day two, John, the seventeen-year old, didn't show up to work, and neither did Jake. Having never faced this before, I felt that I must not have explained the schedule very well, it must be my fault. Mark, the strange one, and Jimmy, the one who wanted my job, did show up. So, I felt that we could get by with production ourselves.

Picture 300 pounds of dough rising in the bowl, Jimmy running back and forth between cutting dough and placing it in the conveyor molder and taking the finished dough balls from the conveyor and placing them into the rotating proof box. Mark, the strange one, was working the oven and I was frantically pressing dough into pizza pans before they over-proofed.

The whole situation got out of control when Mark decided to take a smoke break with an oven full of pizza crusts and with dough balls falling on the floor, while Jimmy was cutting and molding, and I was pressing crusts to try and keep up.

The crusts began to burn and tempers started to rise out of control. When Mark returned, Jimmy started swearing at him and made the mistake of poking him in the chest with his index finger. The next thing I knew, Jimmy was on the floor after being cold-cocked by Mark, the strange one, who still had not said a word.

Day two ended with no usable pizza crusts, a huge personnel problem, an ice pack on Jimmy's right eye, Mark walking out, and a mess that took me well past midnight to clean-up.

This of course went on for a few weeks, with varying degrees of pizza crust success, daily turnover of employees, disgruntled pizza shop managers who were unable to get the crusts they needed, and a bleary-eyed "manager" who was easily working 90 hours per week.

On one of the last days that I remember at King's commissary, I was the only one who showed up. I tried to pull a Lucille Ball "one, man band" routine, but eventually gave up when the dough was over-proofed. Out of frustration, I cut the 300 pounds of dough into smaller units, bagged it up and threw it into the garbage dumpsters outside. The next morning when I returned, the dough had pushed open the fifty pound steel lid on the dumpster and was proofing its way down the driveway.

Salvation arrived that week when my basic training orders came through. I was to leave in three weeks for Fort Jackson, South Carolina for six-months of military training. Frustrated beyond belief, I wrote a note to the owner of King's saying that Uncle Sam called and <u>I am out of here</u>. I taped it to the outside door, locked my keys inside, never picked up my last pay check, and took two weeks off before heading for South Carolina.

Basic Training

The Army is the great equalizer. Rich or poor, educated or not, tall or small, you are all the same in Uncle Sam's eyes. Line-up, extend your arms, receive your neutral clothes, pack your duffle bag, hop on the back of a deuce and a half (that's a 2 1/2 ton truck in military jargon) and off you go to your company bar-racks. Line-up again, stand at attention and wait for the drill sergeant to address the new recruits. First words out of his mouth: The following swinging dicks are scheduled for KP for the first week(that's kitchen police-kitchen grunt workers), Sorgule …, etc.

I was back in the kitchen. Now the Army was never known for the quality of its food or for the skill level of its cooks, so when the company cooks discovered that I had training in restaurants and a college education in the same field, my destiny was set. For the next eight weeks of basic training, I was scheduled every free minute in the kitchen and then spent an additional four months of advanced training as a full-time company cook.

How important is food to a soldier? A German officer following WWII was once quoted to say that it would be hard to imagine defeating an army who is able to provide roast turkey, potatoes, vegetable, dessert and hot coffee to its troops on the front line when we had a difficult time getting bread and water to his. Napoleon stated that an army travels on its stomach. Escoffier, the greatest chef of all time, counteracted the fears and distaste of war by focusing on building spirits among the French troops through the provision of excellent food in the worst of conditions.

Fort Jackson was not the Prussian/French front, but hard days of training were made tolerable with reasonable quality food, served hot and in sufficient quantities. My job as an army cook was gratifying. Although I did not pick up any bulletproof recipes for life, I did enhance my appreciation for the role that cooks play in society.

Aside from the kitchen, the Army experience was unique. I suppose many things seem better the deeper they are imbedded in your past. At the time, the Army training experience was hardly enjoyable. It was something I had to do. There were many parts of the experience that were, well, strange. Common bathrooms without any privacy; room inspections that focused on how you rolled your socks and underwear, and whether or not you could bounce a quarter on the tightness of your bed; spit shined shoes; physical fitness without question; strange foods (some unidentifiable, some indigenous to the South) like grits and hush puppies; 3.2% alcohol beer that allowed men to drink a pitcher or two without any impact except as a diuretic; hand grenade practice (I was a marksman); and the ultimate—the night infiltration course.

The night infiltration course was left for the final week of basic training. A real-life battlefield was designed, including barbed wire, bunkers with dynamite and trip wires, overhead helicopters with spotlights, and live machine gun fire with tracer bullets. We all arrived in full gear, assembled in bleachers and waited for the drill sergeant to brief us. He stood in front of the group and said, "Gentlemen, welcome to the night infiltration course". At that precise moment, dynamite exploded in the bunkers, helicopters buzzed overhead, and rapid machine gun fire broke the silence. We all jumped and broke out in simultaneous cold sweats.

Everyone had to crawl, with their weapons, through the course, which was about the length of a football field. We crawled under barbed wire, around bunkers, watching tracer fire streak over our heads, and occasionally feeling the ground shake when a soldier hit a trip wire and set off a charge. At the end, we all made it through our first "real-life" battle environment and quickly returned to the barracks so we could change our shorts. War is not pretty, and this was as close to the real thing as I wanted to be.

As a cook in the final four months of training, I worked with some great guys. Most of the cooks were army lifers and some of them had recently returned from "Nam." Generally, they didn't like to talk about it, but on occasion I would hear stories of the brutality of combat and the psychological scars that they all shared. More often than not, they would mention how much they liked the innocent civilians of that tropical country. Many of them had severe drug dependencies or at the very least, a definite need to drown their memories with alcohol.

Returning from six months of training, I was back in the job market. The thought of going back to management had been tainted by my experience at King's, but I did give it one more shot. Applying for a position as restaurant manager for a Holiday Inn, I was put through a grueling three-hour interview by the hotel manager. Demeaning would be a great description for this experience, but in the end, the manager gave me some of the best words of advice I had received to this point. "If you want to be a manager, start in the back of the house, learn the kitchen and then move into the role of manager."

Responding to an ad in the paper for apprentice cook, I applied for a position at the Statler Hilton Hotel. This was the first time that I worked for a real chef. The chef was born and trained in Austria, spoke three languages, had worked as executive chef at the Queen Elizabeth Hotel in Montreal and the Hilton in Zurich and was now charged with re-building the culinary reputation of this 1,200-room property. He was again very interested in me, since I had some experience and was trained at a school for restaurant management.

Conrad Hilton and Ellsworth Statler were the two leading players in the development of the American hotel industry. At a point in time, the two merged, forming the Statler Hilton Hotel chain. All of the original Statler hotels were designed identically. The operation in Buffalo was their first. The Buffalo property became the training ground for many of the Statler properties once Buffalo lost its glimmer as a center of tourism on the Great Lakes. In the late sixties and early seventies, the Statler properties offered organized apprenticeship programs for cooks. The program required accepted culinarians to work in all departments of the kitchen as they built their repertoire of skills. I was accepted into this program.

I stayed for six years as a member of the local National Guard unit. I was a cook, of course, in a medical unit. My fellow cooks included Phil (the sergeant), Paul, and a young recruit who we told was on "probation" until he proved himself, so we nicknamed him "Proby". The Guard meets one weekend a month and two weeks each summer for training camp. In essence, we would cook meals on those weekends and when that was complete, we would play cards. When the unit went through summer field training, the cooks got a chance to use the not-so-sophisticated-yet-imaginative kitchen equipment that the Army designed. One such ingenious piece was the industrial-size immersion heater. In order to properly clean and sanitize soldier field utensils, the military used galvanized 50-gallon garbage cans with a unique immersion heater inserted. The heater featured a large metal donut immersed in the can, an attached gasoline tank for fuel, and about 8 feet of smokestack. We used three of these units for each meal—the first for a soapy wash and the last two for rinse and sanitizing.

Proby was really a great guy, but he was often easily misled. We had fun with him, too often at his expense. His jobs were to start up the immersion heaters and fire up the gasoline ranges for cooking. To be prepared for breakfast, he needed to start the immersion units around 5 a.m., while we began cooking. We would sneak out late at night and drip about a 1/2 cup of gasoline into the donut and then shut off the gas tank, leaving just enough gasoline to create a pocket of fumes in the donut.

In the morning, Proby would stumble out of bed, turn the gas tanks on to a drip and blindly insert a flaming torch into the donut to start a small controlled fire. The accumulated gas in the donuts would set off a small but loud explosion, catapulting the smoke stacks off the immersion heaters and waking up the entire unit. We thought it was hilarious—the others did not. Of course, when it works once, you try it again and again, and again. Proby never seemed to anticipate our evil deeds.

What amazed me in the army was how many people said how great the food was. It made me wonder just what they were used to eating. We had significant stores of dehydrated beef, less than stellar vegetables and MSG. Bon appetit!

Up to this point the State of New York or the Federal Government never activated my guard unit. We were activated three times during my tenure for some Acts of God and signs of the turbulent sixties. We wound up in the Southern tier of New York State during severe floods, guarding key locations in Buffalo during the racial riots of that horrible time in our history, and as medical support during the riots at Attica State Prison. I was given a special recognition for service during the Attica riots (my role was to stay 11 miles from the prison and heat up "K" rations for soldiers in our unit in charge of caring for the dead and wounded).

Home, Home on the Range

The kitchen at the Statler Hilton was modeled after the classic brigade of Escoffier with defined departments in butchery, stocks and sauces, baking and pastry, garde manger and hot food preparation. The hotel featured three full-service restaurants and 17 banquet rooms, ranging in seating capacity from 2,000 to 20. I was in awe and a bit nervous.

Everyone seemed to know what he or she was doing. The volume of food preparation was expansive and the skill mastery of everyone was inspiring. The butcher was born and trained in France. He had lived in the United States for over 15 years and refused to learn how to speak English. He was aptly called, "Frenchy". The pastry chef was Italian. He had worked at this hotel for 40 years, making tremendous desserts and breads and without a doubt, the best ice cream I had ever tasted. No one knew his real name so he was always referred to as "Patsy." I can still remember making fresh peach ice cream with Patsy. Long before Ben and Jerry's, he was making the real thing. Fresh, ripe Georgia Peaches were blanched and peeled, some was pureed and the rest cut into a small dice for texture. Egg yolks, sugar, vanilla bean, and cream. This product was comprised of nothing unusual, nothing artificial, just down-to-earth great ingredients. The ice cream was to die for and I can still close my eyes and taste it.

The saucier was also Italian. He made outstanding stocks and sauces, but was very protective of his knowledge. The only way to learn anything from him was to peek around corners while he did his magic. Lastly, Don was the banquet chef. I quickly learned that banquets were a different animal from a'la carte restaurants. The organization of banquets was particularly challenging at the Statler Hotel, since many times all 17 banquet rooms would have events taking place. Don was perfect for the job and was the most interesting and unusual employee that I had ever worked with.

Don was father of 10 children (that's right, 10!). Where he found time for procreation at this level is hard to imagine, since he easily worked 100 hours per week. His routine was well defined. Don arrived at work at around 7 a.m. with a shopping bag in arm. He walked back to his locker in the rear of the kitchen and unloaded two six-packs of beer and a quart of vodka. He then went quickly to the liquor cabinet in the pastry room, grabbed a bottle of rum, poured four shots and knocked them back to help bring a little color to his face and rid himself of the cold sweats. Throughout a full day of massive and skillful production, Don would drink two six-packs of beer and the bottle of vodka. I never saw him drunk.

This brings up the basis for a future interesting study. The number of chefs and managers whom I worked with over the years who had alcohol dependence is frightening. The question in my mind has always been whether or not the job drives people to drink, or the work attracts people who have already been driven to drink. In any case, it is very accessible in restaurants and for years was considered the rule rather than the exception.

In my early days at the Statler, the Executive Chef would issue the cooks a beer ration at the beginning of the evening. The theory, of course, was that we would sweat it out anyway, so no harm done. Alcohol was always the reward. Pay scales were not great, working conditions were industrial, the hours on the job were excessive, and the pressure of the clock was always looming over our shoulders. Ah … a couple of beers and all is forgotten. Great, except many of those whom I worked with could not stop at a couple, and some, like Don, eventually die from over-consumption.

An interesting thing happened during the first week that I was on the job. The chef asked me to prepare him dinner. A shipment of lobsters had just arrived so I anxiously prepared Lobster Thermidor, intent on impressing my boss, the first real chef that I had ever worked for.

Later that day I was looking for the chef regarding a preparation question, when I ran into Don, who told me that the chef was just taken to the hospital. As it happened, the chef had an allergic reaction to shellfish and needed immediate medical attention. Imagine, the first week on the job and I had put my boss in the hospital. Panic and self-doubt almost led me to run from the job. Fortunately, the chef called to say he was fine and that he had experienced similar reactions in his past, but thought that since it had not occurred in quite some time, he was safe. It was his fault, not mine.

Life in the sub-subterranean kitchen of the Statler Hotel (two floors beneath the dining room) was enlightening. This is where I got my first real feel for what a professional (using that term loosely) cook does and how the classic kitchen brigade established by Escoffier at the turn of the century really worked. The chef was the almighty ruler of a pack of diverse, hard working, somewhat strange, occasionally dangerous, characters. Cooks, as I would learn, were much like the pirates I had read about as a child: sinister one moment and kind and comforting the next.

ESCOFFIER'S BRIGADE
EXECUTIVE CHEF

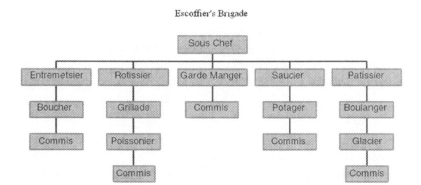

Escoffier's Brigade

Sous Chef:	Production Manager-Second in Charge
Entremetsier:	Prep cook-assembly of station mise en place
Boucher:	Butcher
Commis:	Assistant to …
Rotissier:	The Roast Chef-Hot Food Preparation and Finishing
Grillade:	Grill work-broiler, saute, and deep fry
Poissonier:	The Fish Cook
Garde Manger:	The cold food chef-canapes, hors d' oeuvres, appetizers, cheeses, salads
Saucier:	Stocks and Sauces
Potager:	The Soup Cook
Patissier:	The Pastry Chef
Boulanger:	Baker of Breads
Glacier:	Ice creams and frozen desserts

My job quickly changed. At the time, I was convinced it was because of my culinary competence, but in reality it was because the chef needed people who would show up, suit up, and work whatever hours he deemed necessary. I was promoted to "night chef." Sounded good. This meant that my shift began at 2 p.m. and ended at 11 or 12. I was responsible for preparing hot food from an a la carte menu for the Beef Baron Restaurant. This was the fine dining operation for the Statler Hotel.

I would arrive at two, review anticipated house counts for the evening to determine production, write out a requisition for supplies from central receiving, place the order and wait for delivery from the house steward. Mise en place (preparation—everything has a place and everything is in its place) was fairly routine. Prep for the a' la carte menu, design the night's specials, select a rice and potato of the day, clean my station, organize the cooler, and wait for the orders to arrive.

On days when not scheduled for the evening line, I would also work banquets with Don. At times this was fun, but mostly large banquet work resembles functioning as a member of a factory crew. There were prime rib banquets for 2,000; chicken cordon bleu for 500; small parties of hors d' oeuvres; and an occasional buffet with platters of anything and everything that could be drawn from the coolers.

There were so many behind the scene "events" that distinguished each individual banquet, but a few always stuck in my mind. There was the party for 1,400 New York strip steaks, cooked to varying degrees of doneness. It was beyond my ability to understand how this could be done. The chef, however, was a seasoned problem solver. True, the kitchen only had two broilers with a capacity of approximately 20 steaks at a time, each, but the chef had another idea.

The kitchen featured an island of ranges with flat tops. A flat top was a solid metal plate range with extreme BTU output gas flames underneath. Normally, this was a great surface for saute work and moderate capacity sauce work. The ten ranges could produce some incredible amounts of heat. For the entire day prior to the steak event, the chef had Dominick, the pot washer, scrub and prime these tops until they glistened.

The day of the event, every cook on shift was immersed in a production task that resembled working in the heart of Dante's Inferno. The ranges were cranked up, the flat tops were lightly oiled, the steaks were generously seasoned, and then all were seared to a rich golden color on top of the range.

Flames were shooting three to four feet in the air, smoke filled the kitchen, utility employees stood by with portable fire extinguishers, sweat poured off of my head and the heads of my fellow pirate cooks, smoke filled our eyes and pores, but in a matter of 20 minutes, 1,400 steaks were seared on all sides, lined up, on end, in roasting pans, and readied for final cooking in ovens when the time drew near.

Some pans were dedicated to rare, medium rare, medium, and God forbid, well done. When the function came to a close, it felt like the crew had been through war. The customer was totally oblivious to the method of production or the unique teamwork that was needed to pull it off.

On another typical day when every square inch of the kitchen was dedicated to the all-American banquet: prime ribs, baked potato, green beans amandine—every one of the 17 banquet rooms were full. The Grand Ballroom was filled with 1,200 hungry guests, and the 16 ovens in the kitchen were filled with 22-pound prime rib roasts. Since we could not fit all the roasts necessary to serve 1,200 people in the ovens on hand, we would start roasting at 6 a.m., cook the ribs to blood-rare, move them to warmer boxes that lined the walls of the banquet kitchen, and let them continue to slow cook until service time (a practice that today would be frowned upon). Another batch of ribs was ready for the oven whenever a previous batch was moved to warmers.

Alphonse was one of the banquet cooks. A great guy, Alphonse was Italian and about the same height as me (5 foot 5 inches). Six of our ovens were stacked deck units. So the top oven was above Alphonse shoulder height. He was pulling a strap pan with 44 pounds of rare ribs from the oven when a loose strap caught the edge of the oven door and about two quarts of boiling hot beef fat poured over his chest. I never heard anyone scream so loud.

In the back of the kitchen was a very large cold bain-marie. This is a water bath with refrigeration pipes running under the water line. The unit was used to quickly cool down stocks and sauces before they were moved into refrigeration. Two of us grabbed Alphonse and tossed him into the bain marie to stop the burn from moving deeper through layers of skin. The ambulance was there shortly and Alphonse was taken to a burn unit at Buffalo General Hospital. Fortunately, the second-degree burns only blistered and scarred, but did not debilitate this macho Italian cook. He was back to work in two weeks.

Other occasions included preparing hollandaise sauce for 1,000 orders of fresh asparagus. This delicate emulsified sauce is normally prepared a' la minute (in the moment) in small quantities. The chef showed us how to prepare it in a 60 quart Hobart mixer with a can of sterno underneath as a source of heat. Hundreds of eggs, 50 pounds of clarified butter, dozens of fresh lemons, salt to taste and generous amounts of Tabasco later, I was the new king of hollandaise.

One day when I arrived at work to prepare for my normal shift on the line of the Beef Baron, the chef called me into his office.

"I called in a replacement on the line tonight. I have a special assignment for you."

What could it be?

"The Western New York Republican Party is hosting a fund-raising dinner for election of local officials. There are 1,200 reservations and the guest speaker is Vice President Agnew. The Secret Service has been in the hotel all day and they insist that Mr. Agnew's food be prepared separately, under their constant supervision. I have selected you for this task. You will be working in one of our small banquet kitchens upstairs."

I was honored; of all the cooks in the kitchen, the chef had selected me for this task. Obviously, my skills as a culinarian had impressed the chef so much, that he was willing to pass this very important job to me. I would later find out that I was the only cook on duty that day who passed the Secret Service security check.

Many of the large banquets we served utilized Russian Platter Service. Hot empty plates were presented to the guest and a server, using a spoon and fork held like chopsticks, would transfer the meat, starch, vegetable and sauce work onto the plate in front of the guest. It was fascinating to watch. The skill level of these servers was first rate. What the guest never realized was that these servers were usually from a TEMP service in town. The banquet captain would simply order a number of servers on a need basis.

The dessert of preference for these types of events (usually parties over 500) was Baked Alaska. Baked Alaska a'la Statler style was genoise, topped with Strawberry and Pistachio Ice Cream and finished with beautifully piped Swiss Meringue. At the moment of service, the servers would line-up with logs of Baked Alaska coated with granulated sugar on silver trays. At the last moment, the maitre'd would turn off most of the lights in the ballroom, douse the Baked Alaska with heated brandy and torch the dessert. The servers would parade around the ballroom with blazing Baked Alaska before moving on to their station, where they would slice and serve this elegant dessert. Nearly every event that this was served at was greeted with a standing ovation from the guests.

Line work was fun. I sensed a level of importance and power, particularly over the service staff. My word was final, unless of course, the chef was still at work. The chef had told me in the beginning that when he left, I was in charge. He gave me his phone number, but said don't ever call me unless the place is burning down. He added, "in fact, don't even call me if it is burning down". I took him seriously.

One particular evening was quite slow. Only some 20 odd rooms in the 1,200-room hotel were booked, so pantry person, a dishwasher and me were the only staff on. Mise en place for a slow night like this was nearly non-existent. This was a good time to take care of some extra cleaning, or maybe a little reading.

It was very foggy that night in Buffalo. The airport shut down, canceling all flights, including those connecting flights passing through. The airlines had a standing relationship with the Statler Hotel. In situations such as this, the airport would register customers in the hotel and cover their dinner and breakfast expenses. On this particular evening, this involved nearly 300 stranded, very irritated flyers.

The hotel quickly went from 20 rooms to nearly 200. All these unexpected guests decided to come to dinner at the same time. Even the best-designed plans can sometimes go astray when a curve ball is thrown. Needless to say, we did not have a plan.

The dining room was severely under-staffed, I was not prepped for a crowd, the dishwasher (who we will talk about later) was of no help at all, things happened so fast that calling in reinforcements was not practical and so came the onslaught of orders. I reached a point of total chaos in just a few short minutes. The only logical solution was to make sure the broiler was full of steaks and chops, that shrimp was pre-cooked and ready for finishing sauce work, trays of bakers were slung into 500 degree ovens, and leftover prime ribs from last night's banquets were quickly sliced and dipped in heated au jus. During the beginning stages of battle, I sliced off the top of my thumb. Wrapping my hand in a somewhat clean towel, I continued to cook something and everything.

During the frantic evening of survival cooking, I never figured out if people actually got what they ordered, or for that matter what ever happened to that 1/4 inch piece of thumb.

At one memorable point, the new maitre 'd, Alec, a six-foot, four-inch black man with shoulders out of the NFL and a fairly subdued state-of-mind, considering the circumstances, stood across the line from me and said, "Excuse me chef, can you answer a question for me?"

I returned, "I'll be with you in a minute."

Shortly after, the maitre d' again said, "Chef, can I ask you a question?"

I responded with a bit more accentuation, "I said, I'll be with you in a minute." A third request came from the dead ringer for Mr. T. Now, it is important to understand the psyche of a typical line cook. Most are overly self-confident, totally convinced they are always right, and always free with their comments and language. My response was typical of a chef under duress, "Take your question and shove it up your ass!"

Alec walked around the steam table, grabbed me by the front of my blood stained chef's coat, picked me up with feet dangling, cocked his fist and prepared to pummel this arrogant cook into a pile of leftovers. I saw my life flash before my eyes. My throbbing thumb wrapped in a semi-clean towel, no longer was the focus of my attention, nor were the piles of steaks and shrimp over cooking on the broiler and flattop, all my attention was focused on that monstrous fist waiting for its prey.

Fortunately, Alec was more of a gentleman than me. He withdrew his fist, let go of the chef's coat, backed away while uttering a few profanities and went back to his dining room. In a few moments I regained my composure and somehow managed to plate up the balance of the dinners for the evening.

Note on human relations issues: never allow your mouth to work faster than your brain. In the absence of a brain, keep your mouth shut at all times, and finally, pay special attention to the recipient of your comments.

The next day, I struggled with whether to return to work or simply fade into the sunset. I managed to muster up the courage to return and apologize to Alec. We actually became friends and managed to laugh about the situation after the dust settled.

Occasionally, a celebrity would grace the hotel with his or her presence. The most memorable during my tenure was Elvis. He and his entourage booked an entire floor of the hotel and prohibited access to the floor by anyone not approved by their security force. Elvis was in-house for a few days in preparation for a show in Buffalo. He used a small banquet room off the kitchen for rehearsal, and other than moving from his room to this location, was never seen anywhere in the hotel. I did cook him a late breakfast one morning (poached eggs, if I remember correctly); he sent them back, twice. I never bought another Elvis record.

A final, yet truly enjoyable story occurred one evening when I was again left in charge, but with a few more staff members. A line cook and pantry person was on board, as were two dishwashers and another cook, to help me with a small banquet on the 3rd floor. Since the dessert for the function was Baked Alaska (ice cream and meringue), I told the line cook to send the dessert up to the third floor once I called for it. Might as well keep it nice and frozen until the last minute. I called and after ten minutes was frazzled when the Baked Alaska had not arrived.

I called again, NO answer! I ran down the stairs to give the cook a piece of my mind, only to find that the hot line was on fire. Apparently, the deep fryer caught and flames leapt up the back wall and through the hood system. At one point, flames could be seen lapping out the hood vent on the roof of the hotel.

The fire department was there shortly and the fire was contained after pouring substantial water and chemicals into the line, forcing the closure of the restaurant for the evening. Remembering the chef's initial warnings, I did not call him at home. Instead, the chef found out when he arrived the next morning to a kitchen with an inch of water on the floor and a hot line out of commission.

Note on communication issues: when a chef says don't call me even if the place is on fire, don't believe him. What he really means is don't set the place on fire, but if you do, I want to be the first to know so that I can map out my excuses for the general manager.

By the way, when the Baked Alaska was eventually served that evening flambé' took on a whole new significance.

Just a quick note on the trusty dishwasher: there is no one person, let me state that again-no one person who is more important to the operation of a kitchen, than the dishwasher. If you don't believe it, think of this. If a cook fails to show up, the crew will bitch and moan, but the job will get done. If the chef doesn't show up, the crew will cheer. If the dishwasher doesn't show up, the place falls apart because no one wants to wash dishes, no one except Dominick.

Dominick had washed dishes and pots at the Statler Hotel for more than 10 years. Get that, 10 years! The half-life of most dishwashers was measured in weeks, not years. Dominick lived in a shabby apartment with three other guys, presumably somehow related. Together, they owned one beat-up Studebaker and rarely had enough money to pay for gas. Dominick was flat out crazy. He talked to himself all day long. Many times he would laugh out loud at something that nobody else understood, but we *never* ran out of clean plates, sauté pans, pots, roasting pans, or utensils when Dominick was on shift. Crazy or not, he was always there (at least physically) and he got the job done.

He wasn't much help on the night of the 300 last minute check-ins, but if you needed pots or pans, stoves scrubbed, or even onions and carrots peeled, Dominick was your man. I got to be friends with Dominick and would occasionally pass him a steak or order of shrimp. A way to a dishwasher's heart is through his stomach.

Note on dishwashers: TAKE CARE OF THEM!

I worked with two sous chefs while at the Statler. The first was an idiot. His culinary skills were fair, but his people skills were horrible. He was one of those people who allowed a position to make them feel important. He was missing two fingers on his right hand. Rumor had it he lost them in an accident in another Statler kitchen, and being the sous chef in our shop was a way to keep him from suing the company.

The second sous chef was an intense, hardcore chef with limitless energy, numerous battle stories, and a magnetism that attracted lots of young women. He was the first person to introduce me to carving ice (on my own time, not on the clock), and always leaned on me when it was crunch time in the kitchen. He only stayed a year and was then offered a job as the Executive Chef at a Hilton in Atlanta, Georgia. After he was there a few months he called and offered me the job of sous chef. He flew me down to Atlanta to take a look.

Picture this: I was 21 years old, tired of living in Buffalo, seasoned in the kitchen, fairly confident with my skills, through with Army Basic Training, but totally unfamiliar with living in another part of the country. The thought of moving was exciting and scary at the same time.

The chef (unfortunately, I can't remember his name) had a welcome all planned out for me. I was to stay in the Hilton but would meet him at his apartment, directly behind the hotel. What he did not tell me in advance was that the first two floors of this apartment building were reserved for Delta Airlines as lodging for young women going through their flight attendant training program in Atlanta. It certainly seemed to me like this could work out.

He took me on a tour of underground Atlanta with its clubs and restaurants, introduced me to his friends outside of work, and dropped me back at the hotel. The next day I was to tour the kitchen, get a feel for the operation, and interview with the general manager.

I arrived in my starched whites the next day, only to be greeted by the toughest crew of seasoned cooks I had ever seen. They were not shy about their feelings regarding a young, short, Yankee coming into their kitchen. My hopes of being greeted with open arms were quickly dashed. I turned down the sous chef job and got on the first plane back to Buffalo. Maybe I should have taken the job, but my life (it might have been shortened significantly in Atlanta) would certainly have been different and probably not as gratifying as it turned out.

After two years of interesting exposure to the dynamics of hotel kitchen work at the Statler Hilton, I needed a change. I applied for a job as assistant manager in a college food service. A step in a different direction, maybe the experiences of hotel life had prepared me for management again.

To manage or not to manage, that is the question.

Transitioning from chef's whites to a jacket and tie seemed unnatural. I approached my new job with a bit of trepidation. First of all, these were not real cooks. None of the people working in the kitchen were trained to be professional culinarians. They didn't even wear the right uniform. They didn't swagger around the kitchen as if they were God's gift to mankind, they rarely swore, none of them appeared to be alcoholics, everyone spoke English, the place was very clean in comparison to hotel kitchens, the dishwashers were called "warewashers" or "sanitary engineers," they didn't talk to themselves, and most everyone seemed fairly *nice*.

Of course there are always exceptions. One was an honest-to-goodness cook by the name of Haddie. Haddie had worked at this facility for more than 15 years. She knew her stuff. She always arrived early, she was organized, and she always completed her work on time. The food was not of the same caliber as hotel food, but it was still good.

Haddie didn't talk much, but she was pleasant. I would always say good morning and good night and she would respond in kind. This limited conversation continued for some time until every few months' things would change subtly. Instead of a good morning response from Haddie, she would begin to simply grunt or nod her head. I learned this was a telltale sign of a calm before the storm. In her added silence, Haddie was really waving a flag saying, "I'm pissed off and sooner or later you will feel my wrath." The eruption would usually come within a week of the silent treatment. When it happened, the best one could do was to go along for the ride.

Haddie would grab my arm and drag me into the walk-in cooler. She would then proceed to tell me, in no uncertain words, that I was an idiot, was incompetent, had no business being a manager, and was totally unaware of what was happening in her world. To counteract would only bring more wrath, so I would simply listen and nod my head. After five to ten minutes of this assault, Haddie would nod her head and retreat. I would need a few minutes to regain my manhood and would eventually leave the walk-in and hide in my office. Haddie was back to normal for at least another few months.

I had my first real experiences with unions while in this management role. As a hotel cook, it was always made apparent that everything in a kitchen was everyone's job. Cooks would mop floors, chefs would peel carrots, line chefs would work banquets, and the butcher would even help out the pastry chef on occasion. In this contract food service venue, everyone had a job description and they lived by it. "Not my job" was a common response to directives, which quickly became requests, which eventually became a lost cause. If it wasn't in the job description you could not make them do the work.

Occasionally, I would get the urge to put on whites and step into the kitchen to cook. Not possible! If I, as a manager, was cooking, that meant that someone else was not getting the hours for pay that they deserved. Violate this and the union would breathe down my neck. People did not work more than 40 hours per week. They always got their breaks regardless of how many customers were waiting for food, and rate of pay had little to do with performance, it was dependent on seniority.

I was frustrated. I had to learn an entirely new method of operation, one that was very foreign to me. These "institutional restaurant" employees, although nice people, were not serious about food. They didn't know a chestnut roux from cornstarch, couldn't proclaim the value of caramelization to bring out the flavors in meat, couldn't be bothered with preparing stocks for soups and sauces when all you needed was one of those salty food bases, and thought that fresh-frozen and fresh were exactly the same.

Question: Isn't fresh-frozen an oxymoron?

Students were captive clients. They complained all of the time, but no one really listened. The food was mediocre at best, and that was just the way it was. When the customer was really upset they would stop going to eat. This was actually perfect for the food operator who worked off the benefits of missed meal factor. Since students paid a flat rate for their food service option during a semester, when they didn't show up, they were in essence paying for nothing. Missed meal = profit!

The two redeeming qualities of the job were regular hours for the first time in many years, and lots of young college girls around all of the time. I actually hired one such student, Sharon, who eventually became my wife and better half just two years later.

During my time as a manager at Buffalo State College, I was given responsibility for the operation of a government-subsidized cafeteria for elementary school children, the college pub which dramatically expanded its services with the addition of a pizzeria and live entertainment, the college bowling alley and pool hall, a cash food operation for commuter students, and a deli and contract residence hall cafeteria. In a two-year period, I was exposed to almost every area of food service operation on this sizeable college campus.

Seeing the Light

I was born and raised a Catholic. The nuances of religion were a part of my early life, including one year of Catholic high school. Although I always considered myself to be "God—fearing," I was not consistently passionate about my beliefs. Sharon changed all of that.

In an effort to learn how to understand and become closer to the girl who would eventually marry me, I expressed an interest in her beliefs. These were the 1960's, a time of discovery and a time when many people craved some type of enlightenment. Sharon and I became active members of a spiritual movement. This would lead us to live in a communal school environment in Canada, working with wayward young people, teaching them about farming, cooking, and community.

For six months, Sharon and I worked and lived at Twin Valley's on their organic farm, ran the kitchen operations that fed approximately 200 students and spiritual facilitators, and helped to change the lives of some pretty screwed-up kids. The work was exhausting since we were available to these needy students 24 hours per day. There were 15 year-old drug addicts, young teenage girls who had been arrested for prostitution, and even a young boy who kind of adopted us. We later found out that his crime was attempted manslaughter. After our six-month visa expired, Sharon and I and our dog, Enoch, packed our bags and returned to the States.

Back to my Roots

No jobs, little money, few commitments, and an open mind. Where will all of these factors take a person next? Sharon and I found ourselves back in the Adirondacks. Why? Because of the mountains, the tranquility, a residual grass-roots philosophy carried from the Canadian commune, a sense of familiarity, and the knowledge that the attractions of the mountains to tourists would mean plenty of restaurants to work in.

Sharon, a registered dietitian, had no problem finding a position in a hospital. In fact, her job was secure before we even arrived. Yes, both Sharon and I were immersed in the food business, likely one of the initial attractions that we had for each other.

I took a week to prepare, but landed a job as sous chef within the first five days in the Adirondacks. The property I chose to work at (isn't it interesting that chefs like to choose a property, the property doesn't choose them) was an established, rough-cut gem. Having been a Mecca for serious tourists for a generation, the Mirror Lake Inn was only in need of a fresher, more contemporary approach to food to build its reputation to the next level.

Interviews are an interesting part of life. In essence, the interviewee is attempting to sell himself, while the property is solely trying to avoid making a serious mistake. The interview at the Mirror Lake Inn (MLI) was different. Neither party was really in control, both were simply trying to ascertain whether or not there was chemistry.

The manager, later to become owner, was interesting, tough, determined to raise the bar, and a tad bit intimidating. These characteristics, over the years would lead the MLI to a status of excellence that would not only define the property, but would also create a commitment to excellence in the entire town. I was proud to be a part of it.

Two and a half years of immersion in this firm from the job of sous chef, to bar manager, to chef, to restaurant manager, left an indelible mark on my professional life. In the early days, excellence was measured by doing extraordinary things with very little money. Today, the property invests substantial capital in the process of striving for an even higher level of excellence. What seemed to be the mantra during my tenure with the company was: "We have done so much for so long, with so little, that it seems we can do almost anything with almost nothing."

There were difficult times in the beginning and great learning opportunities as well. Extending credit with purveyors to 90 and 120 days because cash flow was weak, sitting down with the bookkeeper and attempting to determine who must get paid this week to avoid C.O.D. were very difficult decisions, yet life lessons for any chef or restaurateur.

One very difficult night to remember focused on the "lonely diner." It is important to note that in the role of executive chef, I had a real burning desire to inflict my optimum menu on the public at large. Given free reign to design a menu that would put the restaurant on the map, I proceeded to design the mother of all menus—forty of the classics from veal oscar to tournedos rossini, from lobster thermidor to bouillabaisse, from shrimp St. Tropez to baked aubergine (eggplant)—the menu had it all.

The servers were top-shelf and the kitchen was full of the typical borderline crazies that I was used to working with. The location was great from the standpoint of ambience (located directly on the lake), but problematic from a transient business perspective. It was just far enough away from Main Street, Lake Placid that the average tourist could never find it.

On this particular night, the fire was lit, the view over the lake was spectacular, the wines were begging to be opened, and the cooks were ready, willing and able. The only thing lacking was customers. That night we served one lonely diner. The poor guy may have had great food and attentive service, but he surely lacked any real dining experience.

The next day we had a crisis management meeting with me; Lynn, the dining room manager; the owner and his wife. After brainstorming all potential solutions we came up with a real winner. We would run an off-season menu sale! Think about it, other businesses run sales, why not a restaurant? The next day we reprinted menus with the prices crossed out and the new discounted price of $5.95 in place. That's right, $5.95 for Veal Oscar and Lobster Thermidor and all the other 38 items.

We placed an ad in the paper. The first night after advertising we served 50 customers. All right, success! The second night we served 250 guests. The dining room only sat 90, so three turns in a fine dining restaurant. The average wait was 2 hours, but our bar was really cranking.

The back-of-the-house was in chaos. Never in our wildest dreams did we expect this kind of turnout in the early part of April. Fortunately, people were pretty well juiced before they sat down.

The next night we were ready. Loaded for bear. There is another little interesting detail that made this experience all the more meaningful. Lake Placid in April is a ghost town. In fact, most restaurants close and the owners head south for a month. The few remaining restaurants were barely able to make ends meet and struggled from day-to-day. When we started turning 250 covers, it meant that everyone else was totally empty. I became a marked man, loathed and despised in town.

On one very busy evening in April when we ran out of lobster tails, I had the nerve to call a competitor and ask him if I could borrow a case of tails until my next delivery. He was pretty free with what he called me in that moment.

One evening as I left the restaurant and began the nine-mile drive home, smoke started billowing up from under the car. Apparently someone had stuffed paper between the undercarriage of the car and my catalytic converter. Now I could never prove that it was an angry competitor, but it certainly was a coincidence.

A friend of the owner once told him that he proved that the restaurant could give away food; now he had to demonstrate that he could actually sell it. Our food cost was close to 100% during the sale, but the exposure that the restaurant received was priceless.

It took us two months to ease out of this current state, ending up with a cluster of nightly special discounts between $5.95 and $8.95. The restaurant never did reach its potential, but was able to maintain a respectable level of business after this risky marketing gimmick.

Lake Placid was host to two Winter Olympic Games—1932 and 1980. The community had created a compelling reason for people of sports to visit the area and participate in the Olympic dream. As a resort, the level of quality in lodging had increased significantly from the time I arrived till the present day, yet food had not become a reason for people to visit. It was an amenity for those who were there, but lacked the uniqueness necessary of a food destination. I craved an opportunity to help make a food transition.

A Real Life Shift

As fate would have it, what goes around, comes around. In 1979, I worked six straight months without a day off. My 90-hour weeks were taking a toll on my personal well-being and my family's. Sharon was pregnant for the first time and I was compelled to make a change. One thing was certain; whatever I did had to involve food.

Thoughts of becoming a restaurateur came and went. The desire was there, but the fear of risk and a lack of any funds kept those thoughts in check. Then in the mid-summer months an opportunity arose to return to my alma mater and teach. Forget the fact that I had yet to complete my degree, I had experience and stories to tell, skills to share. Surely that would suffice.

Ironically, the job was mine and I began a new career as teacher and mentor. Now this is not a groundbreaking transition. Most culinary educators today are transients from the professional kitchen. Most will tell you that the thoughts of an easy transition to the classroom are quickly dashed when the chef realizes the following:

- you can't fire students
- you can no longer throw pots and pans, yell and scream, and insist that your way is the only way

- saying that you should do it a certain way because "I said so" is no longer sufficient when students are paying for an education

- although the chef may want to insure that everyone who graduates is competent as he, some will never be

- not everyone wants to be a chef, they simply want to cook

- assumptions are great, but assume makes an "ass of u and me".

I was now a teacher; at least that was what my contract said. Think about this for a moment. Chefs work 70–100 hours per week, six to seven days a week, and rarely get a vacation. Teachers work 30–40 hours per week, five days, and have numerous weeks' vacation during the year. This transition, although it may seem well deserved, is shocking to a chef. Inevitably what happens is that chefs quickly figure out ways to fill up this wasted time with either additional projects related to teaching, consulting, or a second job altogether. The thought of working 40 hours per week is absurd.

I was afraid of boredom, so I quickly took it upon myself to fill in the gaps with meaningful food-related activities. I became obsessed with developing a culinary arts major at my alma mater and developing a vehicle for transforming the Adirondacks into a food destination, as well as a sports destination.

Back to the days when I was working short order with Millie, if a person asked you what you did for a living and you said, I'm a cook, they would likely feel sorry for you. Through the wonders of television, a supportive media, and characters like Julia Child, Jacques Pepin, James Beard and Graham Kerr, cooking became an American obsession.

In the "good old days" people didn't go to school to learn how to cook, they simply started in the dish room and worked their way up the ladder. Most people began with dishes to onions and potatoes, to breakfast, to salads, to hot line, to banquets to sous chef and so on. The culinary world was on the verge of change and the job of chef right along with it.

In 1979, I received State Education Department approval for the first Culinary Arts degree to be offered at Paul Smith's. In all fairness, the initial impetus for this movement came from my early mentor, my first food teacher, Fran Peroni. The initial 23 students were disciples of Child, Beard and Kerr—anxious to learn more about cooking, somewhat turned off by traditional educational programs, but convinced that food was their thing.

I had always thought that I knew a fair amount about food and cooking; my education was only about to begin. I spent 26 years preparing people to become cooks and chefs. The stories are endless, this is just a taste.

2

Teach the Teacher
How Come the Chicken Isn't
Getting Brown?

I had never been classically trained, but quickly realized that if I were to contribute to the education of serious cooks, then I would have to become more serious myself. The kitchens of my past were meccas for protective veterans, degenerate pirates, and innate masters of the kitchen who learned through the school of hard knocks.

Unless you really understand the history of food, the components of a culture, the political and religious influence of food, geography, geology, agriculture and weather, the ability to cook, I mean really cook, is diminished.

To be a teacher, all of those factors are an essential part of your repertoire. The anecdotal experiences of a pirate cook must be supplemented by a stronger foundation in the classics and an acute awareness of what is happening today in kitchens all over the world.

As a program of 23 student explorers continued to grow, so too did the understanding of food grow in their teacher's culinary experiences. What would take place over the next twenty-some years would be truly remarkable. The people I met, the culinary friendships that I built, the students I had the pleasure to work with, and the travels that I took transformed my professional and personal life.

"Why Isn't the Chicken Getting Brown?" There is a statement by either Voltaire or Mark Twain that refers to the fact that common sense is not so common. Teachers and trainers who assume that some things are obvious, are in for a surprise.

Cooks are not born. There is no magic part of the genetic code that differentiates cooks from non-cooks. Some people are truly gifted with better taste buds or olfactory senses, but born a cook? Not likely. Cooks are trained through time, trial and error. In the case of students, lots of time and error.

Learning to cook is one thing; learning to be a cook is something entirely different. I truly believe that anyone can be taught, at varying levels, how to cook. Theoretically there are 290 million potential cooks in the United States. If you have an ounce of common sense and can read, you are *teachable* as a cook. That being said, if it were not for microwave ovens and fast food drive-thrus, a good portion of the population would likely starve. This is not due to a lack of potential, but rather pure, simple laziness.

This, of course, is a topic for another study and multitudes of other articles and books, but it feels good getting that basic belief off my chest. People in America are lazy, very lazy (not everyone, but a fair share)! There, I feel even better. What is even more absurd is that many companies in the food business have been enormously successful having come to this realization. We cater to the laziness of our population.

Back to the original point, anyone can be taught how to cook, but can they be taught how to BE a cook? The cooks and/or chefs that I have alluded to throughout the introduction to this book are unique. Cooks are dedicated, yet unpredictable; trustworthy, yet undependable; passionate about food, yet carefree about their own eating habits. They're also friendly, yet sometimes hard as stone; analytical, yet sometimes too analytical; cooks through training, yet well-tuned production machines in the heat of the moment. And finally, cooks have common sense.

Is it possible then to actually teach people to become cooks and chefs? The answer is simply yes, and no. Yes, if they are willing to understand the complexity of the person and position; no, if they only want to learn how to cook. Can you measure the success of a culinary arts program by how many chefs it trains? The answer is best put in a different context. There are in the neighborhood of 700 culinary schools in the United States today. The number of culinary students in the United States has grown exponentially since the mid-1960's. If every graduate from these schools went on to become a chef, there would likely be more chefs than restaurants.

At Paul Smith's, like many other culinary schools, we strove to build a solid foundation of cooking skills, while exposing individuals to the environment of the cook. In this environment that students can transform from people who can cook, to people who can be classified as cooks. The adage that the best educator is experience certainly applies. What the culinary school can do is lay the groundwork, feed the passion and speed up the transition process.

Two such semesters at Paul Smith's were called the internship and the externship. Often everyone, including the student, confuses these. Simply stated, the internship is "internally" controlled by the college with faculty supervision. The environment is real, but the support mechanism is still a bit surreal. The externship, on the other hand, is a true experiential work semester. The student works for a company or individual property for credit and pay. They are a regular employee who simply receives structured performance reviews and college credit for satisfactory work. The advantage to the property is that they receive an employee who is serious about dedicating their life to this endeavor, and the student gets a chance to observe the inner workings of a real restaurant and to determine if this is what they really want to do.

The stories that go along with these "real-life" experiences are sometimes inspiring, oftentimes comical, and occasionally sad. Case-in-point: I began my teaching career at the college's sole internship site in 1979. The Hotel Saranac was owned and operated by the college. Located in the booming metropolis of Saranac Lake, New York, this 88-room property suffered from seasonalitis. A boutique hotel in a small town can expect about five good business months per year and the balance of the time you try to not lose everything that you have gained.

The Hotel Saranac was not designed to be a profit center, but rather the best possible training site for our students. Can you imagine being faced with the following business scenario? Every one or two weeks, your staff in every department changes. Maintaining a level of consistency becomes a real challenge. Nothing can be assumed. Here is a perfect example: my position at the Hotel Saranac involved preparing students to present a weekly student-run buffet. Depending on the month, this buffet could attract anywhere from 100–400 customers. Every week, I was presented with a new crew, a different theme, a different set of recipes, and a list of unpredictable outcomes.

On one particular day, I had set up a breading station for cornmeal-fried chicken. The theme was Southern U.S. and I prepared a station with seasoned flour, egg wash, and seasoned cornmeal. I partially fried in advance one batch of chicken to demonstrate the color that I was looking for. The intent was that the chicken would be browned and then finished in the oven as demand was placed on the kitchen during the buffet.

I asked the student assigned if he understood the technique of keeping one hand dry for dry ingredients and the other for the egg wash. His response was a clear, "yes!" I pointed out the partially fried chicken and asked if he understood the degree of doneness and color that I was looking for. The response was a resounding, "Yes chef!" I felt good.

I moved out to the dining room to work with some students on the tiering of the buffet line. After about ten minutes, my confident fry-guy came out to the dining room. "Chef, I did what you said, but the chicken isn't getting brown." Of course the typical thoughts went through my head, the breaker must have flipped off on the power panel, or there was something wrong with the thermostat on the friolater. I went to the kitchen to investigate. The fry-guy had properly dredged and breaded the chicken, one dry hand, one wet. The chicken was meticulously placed in the fryer baskets; I checked the breaker—it was on. I checked the pilot light on the fryer, a-ok; I dropped the basket of chicken in the fryer and everything was working just perfectly. In the background I heard, "Oh crap!" Apparently, my fry-guy with a grade point average of 3.0 did not have enough common sense to drop the chicken into the fat. He must have thought that the chicken would brown through proximity.

Rule of the day: don't assume anything.

As an observation over the years, it is ironic that sometimes the students who do not excel in the classroom are very adept at performing in production situations. On the other hand, those who have a long track record of classroom excellence, find the real-life of the kitchen to be very challenging. Go figure.

Sometimes chefs can have fun with students. There is a different aura of respect between students and a chef that is not always present between student and any other teacher. I don't know why that is. Maybe a little fear, hopefully some level of respect, yet there is a difference. I have found over the years, that culinary students, particularly freshmen, will do basically whatever a chef asks without question.

In 1981, I brought a visiting chef from the Birmingham School of Catering in England to the Adirondacks for a month long exchange. He was competent, very tall, and visually intimidating. The British are known for their serious nature and dry sense of humor. This chef was no exception. It was his first trip to the United States and he was a bit taken back when he discovered that we didn't all ride horses and rope steers.

His first encounter with any real Americans happened after his arrival in Saranac Lake during our annual Winter Carnival. Now I have to paint a picture of the local inhabitant of Saranac Lake for you to truly appreciate this first impression.

There are three types of people in Saranac Lake: natives, locals, and transients. Obviously, you need to be born in Saranac Lake to be a native, but you must live there nearly as long to even be considered a local; thus everyone but a few are transients. The town sits within two counties, Essex and Franklin. Both counties have some of the highest year-round unemployment rates in the State of New York, and on the average, very low mean family incomes. Most residents work in hospitality, health care, education, or construction.

The area enjoys one prominent season, winter; and three minor seasons, Mud, Fourth of July and Leaf Peeper season. Actually, the seasons are great; winter is just a bit too long.

Our visiting chef arrived in the middle of winter. The temperature was around 20 below zero, the snow was about four-feet deep, and Saranac Lake was hosting its favorite annual event: Winter Carnival. Saranac Lake hosts the oldest winter carnival in the United States. In mid-February, every local, normal and crazy, is out on the streets, beer in hand, woolen pants and Sorrel boots, and for some reason, a high level of anticipation for the feature event: the Carnival Parade. Now this is, without a doubt, the lamest parade you could ever imagine with synchronized lounge chair marchers, high school bands, floats made by heavily intoxicated people with serious cabin fever, and fire trucks and police cars. All this being said, the parade is a terrific amount of fun.

I picked the chef up in Montreal and let him out in front of the Hotel Saranac bursting with local flavor at the end of the parade. He was in total shock. I can only imagine that first call home to explain where he was and what Americans were really like.

The next Monday, he was hosting his first culinary lab for Paul Smith's freshmen. The task at hand, chopping parsley, cutting carrots into brunoise, and turning potatoes, it was the first day of foundational knife skills. Students were unusually responsive to the chef's orders and anxious to learn the difference between American and British technique. The chef was fully aware of his power over them and told each student to place their right foot behind their left knee while they chopped parsley; this, as he told them, would provide greater leverage for the knife and cleaner cuts on the parsley. Fifteen students were struggling to stand with one foot tucked behind the other knee, concentrating on ways to avoid cutting their fingers off in the process. It was hilarious.

Special note: there are plenty of opportunities for chef instructors to have a good laugh.

Special Events:

One comment from a recruiter always sits in the back of my mind as a real distinction for culinary programs. I asked him why he hired graduates from our school, his response: "Because they are not afraid to work hard." If you were to list the pros and cons of hiring any employee—talented, intelligent, consistent, cooperative, anxious to learn, passionate about food, etc., it would be difficult to place any of those attributes above "not afraid to work hard."

I know that one of the reasons for this comment about these graduates' stems from the schools historical involvement in special events. The College participated with Harry M. Stevens Company in the Kentucky Derby for 20 years, with Restaurant Associates at PGA Golf Tournaments and the U.S. Open Tennis Grand Slam, and the Lake Placid Horse Show events throughout the 80's and 90's.

Special Events Catering is one of the most demanding types of food service requiring incredible stamina, the ability to adjust at a moment's notice, field mentality, and a bit of the "Carny" in you. Kitchens with grass or dirt floors, cooking facilities under tents, walk-in coolers that moonlight as refrigerated delivery trucks, and wiring and plumbing that could be described as "scary" at best.

The Kentucky Derby is the two most exciting minutes of sports every year. In the late seventies, a vice president for Harry M. Stevens (the company who invented the hot dog) and an alumnus were watching the phenomena on the infield and a light bulb went off: "What if we could get a hot dog and a beer into the hand of each one of those people in the infield who are there because they could not afford seats in the grand stands." The next year they began with cases of beer and boiled dogs serving the 80,000 people who crushed into the center field surrounded by the Derby Track. By the time the college became involved they were generating nearly a million dollars in sales in the single afternoon of the Derby.

The sheer volume of business was incredible. Try 900 kegs of beer in one afternoon! I was responsible for introducing the first Chipwich (Ice cream between two chocolate chip cookies) at this event in 1981. I had six sellers at different locations throughout the infield and sold 14,000 of them in one day.

There was a specially designed dispensing system for mint juleps. A Derby souvenir glass was placed in typical dishwasher glass racks, the rack was pushed through a conveyor where a stainless trip bar was pushed, and dispensing just the right amount of bourbon and white crème de menthe mix over crushed ice. The mint julep mix was drawn from stainless soda pre-mix cylinders designed for this event. A sprig of fresh mint and $6 would get the customer a good old southern buzz. People were buying these at 8 a.m. on the day of the Derby. By noon, the entire infield was totally drunk. Talk about chaos.

In the center of the infield were massive flower pedestals, probably ten feet tall. The flowers had been removed for the day, but that didn't stop a 400 pound guy from working his way to the top, turning towards the Southern Belles in the grand stands, dropping his drawers and displaying his unpleasant natural self to the shocked audience. He kept his T-shirt on, which proclaimed, "The Incredible Bulk." The subliminal message here pointed to the socio-economic distinction that was so apparent at this monumental sporting event.

The real education, of course, was learning how to deal with massive crowds of over-served people and moving out incredible amounts of food and beverage in some type of reasonable system.

As massive an undertaking as was the Derby, it paled in comparison to the U.S. Open Tennis Tournament. This was a much classier event, presented over two weeks with dollar figures that would make any other restaurateur shake their head in disbelief. The coordination alone took an entire year.

Restaurant Associates is a class operation. Operator of some of New York's finest restaurants and office food services, RA is the premier specialty restaurant and special event caterer in the United States. The Tennis Open involved focused tent restaurants for high-end clients like American Express and Head Tennis Rackets, Reebok and Nike, and the like; cafeteria style operations for the masses (but not cafeterias as most of us think of them); and Food Village.

Food Village was a cluster of thematic storefront stands that took care of the culinary cravings of 20-plus thousand tennis buffs and players every day. The college worked with RA for nine years, bringing 40 or so students to work Food Village for the two weeks of the event.

Food Village included a Mexican Restaurant, Char-grilled hamburger stand, New York style deli, Italian Tratorria, Baked Potato cart, and one-year, a Buffalo style chicken wing stand.

Most amazing was the hamburger stand. The preparation/service area was about 600 square feet and included two gas char-grills, two deep fryers, 16 feet of stainless table, two beverage coolers, soda dispensers, a double keg cooler, one 8' x 8' walk-in cooler, a double bay sink and dry storage.

Fourteen students worked in this tiny space: six sellers, three grill men, the fry-guy, an expeditor, two prep people, and a supply runner. Once the event started to kick in, the stand was totally maxed out from 11 a.m. until midnight or later for two weeks. On average, the stand would generate between $35,000 and $40,000 per day in sales, keeping in mind that a hamburger was $6.

Production was a real feat. We would go through 40–50 cases of tomatoes, 300 pounds of onions, and 4 to 5,000 half-pound hamburgers every day. Try a little math. The two char-grills could handle a capacity of 64 hamburgers at a time. The flames would shoot 4–6 inches from the top of the grill, as the fat in the burgers would drip on the coals. The smoke was incredible, so much so that one-year they issued gas masks to the grill guys so that they could work through the smog. Finally, the players complained about the smoke until they installed hood scrubbers the next year.

Back to math: On a day when we sold 5,000 hamburgers, we needed to cook 78 batches of patties. If it takes 4–5 minutes on a side for these half-pound burgers to cook, that is 10 minutes per batch, or 780 minutes. That's 13 hours of cooking. Now factor in that continuous quality cooking is probably not going to happen, the grill needs to be scraped down on occasion, and impatient customers are not likely to wait ten minutes for a burger. The end result is lots of rare hamburgers and cooks falling down, left and right.

On my first day there I watched as students were gasping for breath, sweating like Niagara Falls, and looking like punching bags after only 30 or 40 minutes. Of course, I was the seasoned professional so I told them to take a break and I would show them how it was done. After 20 minutes I was sitting down on a milk crate behind the stand, trying to catch my breath and wondering where my youth went. It took me a full hour to recover.

We stayed at a Marriott Hotel on Long Island, about 30 minutes from the Tennis Center. So including the typical 17–18 hour work day and at least 1 hour of round-trip transportation, we were lucky to get 4 hours of sleep each night. After two weeks, we could barely remember our names.

One year when we arrived, I was told that the company was opening its first proto-type Buffalo Chicken Wing stand. My job was to supervise the operation for the first week of the Open and solidify the concept. Since it was to be the next "big deal." every manager with any clout in the company was hovering over the operation as we prepared for the first day of business.

The stand was no more than 400 square feet, including a closet kitchen with four deep fryers, a hand sink, one single door reach-in cooler, and a hood system without a fan, in a closed kitchen without a light. The selling area had soda dispensers and two four-well steam tables to hold mild, medium, and hot and inferno wings. Two cash registers completed the scene. We were ready for business. The menu was simple—wings and soda, but complex in options of sizes and heat.

Now the process of cooking wings is to simply fry them raw until they are crisp, golden brown and thoroughly cooked. The wings are then tossed in their respective sauce and passed on to the steam table. Not rocket science. What went against our success was an underestimation of the volume of wings that people would want, the extensive number of choices on the menu, and a constricted facility.

Two people, an older student who was also from Buffalo and me, manned the kitchen. Just prior to opening on day one, we had the operation loaded for bear. The wings were in their respective steam table homes, the stand was the best it would look for the next two weeks, and I was setting the mise en place in our minuscule kitchen. The other Buffalo student was out front.

Up to the stand came the President of the company, the Corporate Food and Beverage Director (who had designed the concept), the Director of the U.S. Open food program, and the Corporate Chef who had developed the four sauces for the wings.

All four gentlemen asked for samples from the student. After trying the wings the company president turned to the student and asked what he thought of the product. The student started by asking, "Do you want to know the truth?" Before I could leap over the counter to stop him, he blurted out: "These wings suck!" I had instant visions of the company pushing the entire college crew onto the fastest bus home, along with a stinging call to the president of the college. Instead, he responded: "Why do you think they suck?" Our trusty student followed with an explanation: "I'm from Buffalo and the only true Buffalo wings come from the Anchor Bar, where I used to work. If you want authentic Buffalo wings, then you have to use Frank's Hot Sauce." There, he said it. I felt the noose tightening around my neck. The student was oblivious to the mistakes in protocol he had just made.

The president of Restaurant Associates turned to the Food and Beverage Director and said; "Close the stand until we can get Frank's Hot Sauce in." He thanked the student and they walked away. The next day a tractor-trailer pulled up with a pallet of gallons of Frank's Hot Sauce.

Over the next week, the stand was absolutely crazy. The two Buffalonians in the kitchen had burn marks from elbow to wrist, the sheer amount of grease made it impossible to stand upright and we both noticed our skin breaking out like we were teenagers. The heat in the kitchen was unbearable (remember a hood without a fan) and occasional small fires broke out, as grease ignited. Fryers over flowed due to the water content in the wings; the single hand sink became stopped up on day one and never freed up for the entire week. We broke down cardboard boxes to cover the concrete floor in the kitchen and service areas, since the floors were so slick we were literally falling down. Although we should have changed the grease in the fryers twice per day, there simply was not enough time and I refused to change the hot grease at the end of the night. So each morning at 7 a.m. we were faced with fryer grease and chicken fat.

Since there was no light in the kitchen, once nightfall came, the degree of doneness on the wings was always questionable. The volume far exceeded the capacity of a single door reach-in cooler; in fact, we were selling more than 2,000 pounds of wings per day.

The good news was that the stand was very, very busy and the sales volume exceeded the company's expectations. The bad news was that the design of the facility was horrible and unchangeable for the duration of this event.

At the end of the night we all looked like degenerate transient cooks with bloodshot eyes, cracked and bloodied hands, swollen feet, burns up the length of our arms and pores full of grease. Don't even ask how we must have smelled.

The saving grace was that at the end of the evening, as business would start to slow down, we would take turns (the chefs and operation managers) cooking for each other. We shared this routine with the cadre of chefs who worked the high-end tents and specialty events throughout the week. The food was great, the company refreshing, the banter was ruthless, and the jokes made me laugh so hard that I would literally fall out of my chair.

Now I can't really take credit for the full Monty of backbreaking work, because through the five years that I participated, I only worked the first week. Classes for the fall started halfway through the Tennis Open and thank God I had to get back.

The Godfather of the Open was Tim. Tim was an instructor from Paul Smith's who started teaching just two weeks after I did in 1979. Like me, he was a bit burned out from tenure in the hospitality industry. He had great stories, was a magician at networking, could sell you the shirt off your back, and knew how to work the system. He was candidly referred to as the Mayor of Food Village. Whenever the Sports Networks would get tired of covering the matches, they would pay a camera visit to Food Village. Inevitably they would find Tim. He was our spokesperson, the person who was able to convince the world that any level of success that Andre Agassi or Steffi Graf had on the tennis court was due to the quality of our char-grilled hamburgers.

When Tim was on his game, he was masterful at keeping the machine running; when he chose not to be on his game, he was just as masterful at that. The reality is the Open would not have been the Open without Tim.

Others came, burned out and went. Aside from me, there was Chris, who was a breath of fresh air and intense at running the hamburger stand, but who had a difficult time with driving directions. Sense of direction was not her forte. Joel, still my go-to guy and special events problem solver, who combined fast ball pitching with tomato slicing to create the most innovative way of preparing tomatoes for hamburger garnishes that anyone had ever seen. The chefs from corporate tents used to come by to watch him pitch his culinary magic.

Other interesting players included Joe, the almighty leader who ran the whole show. I never knew that the price you paid for products from purveyors was totally negotiable, until I watched Joe wear down a salesperson to the point of tears. Serge was the corporate chef, who could be serious one moment, but lighthearted and carefree the next. It was obvious that Serge had mastered the ability to herd cats, because all of the other chefs either respected him or acted like they did. Dean was the college alum who worked the Open as a student and never left the company. He became the logistics man for this event and numerous others. Finally, Salla, the comptroller who calmly handled the sizeable amounts of cash that flowed in and out of the two-week gold mine business like it was just another day at the office.

There were many other classic events, but let me finish these stories with an event with some local flavor. The Lake Placid Horse Shows are held each year the last week of June and first week of July. These are world-class equestrian events that feature stadium jumping and dressage. If you like watching horses, these animals are incredible, and very expensive.

I was involved with the Horse Shows for six years—once as the Chef at the Mirror Lake Inn and five years with the college. The advantage I had once the college became involved was an army of students.

If sociologists needed a perfect case to study regarding differentiation of classes, the Horse Show was the mother lode. There were the owners and riders, and then there were the people who groomed the horses. My vote went to the groomers. These were real people, people who worked hard for a living, people who were crazy and rarely sober. If anyone walked in from the U.S. Department of Immigration and Naturalization these real people probably would have scattered in every direction.

The groomers appreciated the food we made, were waiting for coffee by 5:30 a.m. and actually spent more money on food than the horse owners and riders did. Actually, there was a real connection between groomers and typical cooks.

Our kitchen in the first few years was a grass floor and trenches around the perimeter to prevent flooding when it rained. Our walk-in was a refrigerated truck from Sysco; wiring was haphazardly laid in shallow trenches (if it wasn't for ground-fault breakers we would have been electrocuted).

The food was simple but fun and our students had a chance to learn about carnival systems and reasonable volume. The deciding factor between success and failure was the weather. Two weeks of sunshine would yield $50,000-$60,000 in sales. Two weeks of rain would be a real disaster.

Students filled in some of the positions required, but area high school students covered the lion's share of jobs. I needed help with limited training, trouble shooting and cash control so I hired my brother-in-law and sister-in-law to cover these areas. They are both elementary school teachers and had summers off. I think they actually had fun.

The last year that I was involved, was the most interesting. The Convention Bureau for Lake Placid had booked another significant event immediately after the Horse shows. With a one-day gap, the Horse shows were to be followed by a BMW Motorcycle rally.

BMW owners are not your typical bikers. These are not Harley Hogs with an attitude of "can't touch me." They are doctors and lawyers driving these beautiful, way too proper bikes. They don't rumble into town, they hum. The village promised 6,000 bikers arriving at the Horse show grounds with their $30,000 machines and lots of cash to spend on food and drink. I took the gig and began the planning for three solid weeks of special events.

One of the logistics problems at the Lake Placid events was delivery of supplies. Since the BMW event, unlike the horse shows, was primarily on a weekend, deliveries were more difficult to arrange. I needed to have all of the supplies on premise before they arrived. Also, since they were less likely to appreciate hamburgers, hot dogs and tacos, the food and the cooking equipment needed to be different.

I designed a cooking pit that was 30 feet long. A cinder block barbeque pit fired by wood and controlled with rakes and asbestos suits. The fire would need to be kept burning round-the-clock.

The horse shows were a given. After five years, planning them was a piece of cake; adding the BMW rally pushed the planning in another direction. I needed more staff to manage the events, including satellite locations to sell quick service items and a portable convenience store to provide cigarettes, cigars, toiletries, candy bars, etc. for these upscale campers. Security would be an issue and a barbeque pit boss with culinary attitude was essential.

I put together an unlikely crew: Ruth, a five-foot powerhouse sous with an attitude would be the kitchen manager; Kevin a 6'5" ex-professional basketball player who played for a team in Finland would be my chief of security; and Rick, a former owner of a garbage collection service-converted to chef would be the "pit-boss" for the blazing cinder block wood grill.

We got through the horse show without any problems; in fact our sales were up 25% from the previous year. The show ended and the horses and their support staff left, giving us one day to convert our facility to accommodate the BMW crowd.

An unforeseen problem reared up its ugly head within hours of the horse's departure. When the horses (all 1,000 of them) were on site, there was virtually no problem with flies, since they like horses. When the equine team left, the flies had nowhere to go except.... .the kitchen! With bikers arriving by the hundreds, I was faced with a dilemma of epic proportions. The flies were so thick you could barely move in the kitchen. I called the exterminator and frantically pleaded for an immediate offensive attack. When he arrived, he was astounded. It was the most severe fly problem he had ever encountered. By the next morning the flies were gone, but it took us the entire evening to sterilize the kitchen facility.

I was ready! We had a 16-wheel trailer filled with produce. Dozens of cases of tomatoes, peppers, cucumbers, onions, and zucchini, red bliss potatoes, peaches, plums, apples and fresh cherries. You name it—we had it. Next to the produce truck were two bread trucks filled to the brim with rolls, loaves of bread, English muffins, danish and donuts. We would not have to worry about weekend deliveries.

The pit crew was ready, masked in asbestos suits that we borrowed from the local fire department. The pit had been burning down to coals since the night before. Custom-made grills with 2-foot handles for turning were burned off for sanitation. The BMW motorcyclists had arrived, nearly 6,000 of them.

Our first night's menu featured teriyaki Cornish game hens. The 30-foot pit was covered with hundreds of split hens. Bring on the crowds! The only problem was they had no desire to spend $10 for outdoor cooking, when dozens of Lake Placid Restaurants were just down the street. We sold less than 100 dinners that night.

Panic struck as I quickly realized I had been severely misled by an ill-informed visitor's bureau and I was looking at massive amounts of leftover food and diminished sales. At the end of the event, we had lost everything we had gained from a terrific horse show and I was looking at tractor trailers full of food.

My staff and I spent the next two days as door-to-door salesmen, selling extra produce, breads and staples to area restaurants at 10 cents on the dollar in an attempt to minimize the loss.

Lesson: Don't place your trust in second-hand speculative data. If you are considering contracting with a large event, do your own research first.

3

Becoming a True Culinarian

Up to this point I had always considered myself a chef and a manager by trade who happened to work as a teacher. I was about to experience a tremendous professional change.

Food started to become even more important in my life, particularly my professional life. The amount of time I spent in front of a range had actually decreased, but my breadth of knowledge about food, the process of cooking, the history of food and culture, and the future of the industry were increasing exponentially.

You can't teach students about cooking and becoming a chef unless you know far more about it than the student needs to be exposed to. I was able to increase my understanding of food through reading and attending trade shows, through membership in organizations like the American Culinary Federation, the National Restaurant Association, the Research Chefs Association and through involvement in culinary competitions.

Actually, the first competition that I entered was in Buffalo, New York when I was 20 years old. I made Paella Castellana in a huge 36-inch diameter Paella pan. That was different. There were very few parameters for competitions in those days.

I entered my first competition as a culinary educator in 1981 in Buffalo. I worked within the guidelines compiled by the ACF, spent time designing a menu, worked out production sheets, prepared and haphazardly made my first attempt at glazing with aspic, and set up my table at the show sponsored by the Buffalo Chapter of the ACF. I won a bronze medal and I was hooked.

Over the next five years, I entered 16 shows, constantly improving my research and my skills as a competition chef. I won gold, silver and bronze medals, a few first place trophies and even two best of show. I was able to pass on a better understanding of food in my classes and dramatically raised the bar in terms of perfecting my food presentations.

In 1986, I received a call from a great chef friend, Anton Flory. Tony was one of the first five Certified Master Chefs in the United States, a chef at a premier property in nearby Vermont, and an absolutely wonderful human being. His call took me totally by surprise. "Paul, we are trying to put together a team of chefs to represent New England at the Culinary Olympics in Frankfurt, Germany. I think that you should tryout for one of the slots on the team." I was silent. Of course I wanted the opportunity, but I did not feel that I was ready for the challenge. "Tony, I am honored, but don't you think this is out of my league?" When he reiterated that he wouldn't ask me unless he thought that I was ready, I accepted the challenge.

The tryouts were held in Boston in April of that year. Paul Smith's would be there anyway since I had taken a team of students to compete at the Northeast Food Service Show each year since 1980. I asked another faculty member to focus on our student team as I began to compile my research for a tryout presentation. I only had a month to prepare.

The day of the tryout, I laid down my menu program, stepped back, and assessed it at a grade of "C", it was fun to try, but I felt that it just wasn't good enough.

A week later, I received a call at home from Chef Flory. "Paul, this is Tony. Congratulations, you made the team! We are going to announce the entire group at a reception in Boston in two days. Can you make it?" I was in shock. Actually, a bit weak in the knees, but I said "YES!"

At the Ritz Carlton in Boston, Tony, the local press and our guest of honor, Julia Child, greeted me. The ten-team members (who were strangers to me) posed for group photos and shook hands with those dignitaries in attendance. Tony pulled us aside and said that he had selected one team member as a captain. The captain would set the process in place and give the team the direction we needed to get to Frankfurt. Roland was the man.

Roland was born and trained in Austria. He was a talented, self-confident, strong-willed chef with the right amount of intensity to pull this off. Roland was the Executive Chef at the Park Plaza Hotel in Boston, ironically an old Statler Hilton Hotel that was a mirror image of the Buffalo Statler where I got my real start. I was intimidated not only by Roland, but by the entire group. What gave me the right to be here?

The other chefs were just as impressive as Roland. Danny, I would discover, was a perfectionist and a seasoned veteran in the competition arena. Jose' was the Chef Garde Manger at the Ritz in Boston and seemed very comfortable as a member of this elite group. Lars was the elder gentleman of the group, without a doubt one of the most respected pastry chefs in the world. Lars was Swedish-born and trained as a veteran of Olympic competitions. Lars was the director of the pastry school at Johnson and Wales. Neil was the consummate Irishman—a chef and pastry chef, with tremendous confidence without any swagger. He had a reputation for tremendous chocolate centerpieces at competitions in the New England area. Neil was the Executive Chef for the Kennedy family at their compound. I took an instant liking to George. He was quiet, but sincere. He seemed as uncomfortable with this challenge as I did, but since he worked with Lars, he at least had a mentor to lean on. Mickey was the light-hearted glue that held the team together. He was a seasoned executive chef and in awe of the opportunity that was before him. Walter was the one chef who seemed to feel that he belonged. He was apparently well connected in the Boston culinary scene and knew Julia Child better than anyone else in the group. He was chef at the Charles Hotel in Cambridge. The last team member would later leave our group due to conflicts with his job, but would be replaced by Charles, who I will talk about later in this chapter.

Roland had a quick meeting with the group and said that we would likely meet a few times to plan and then two or three times to practice before Frankfurt in October of 1988. It seemed like a reasonable schedule. Our first meeting would be in a few weeks at his home. We were to bring preliminary sketches of pieces that we would like to make for the competition so that the group could discuss them. I left feeling a bit more comfortable.

The process of becoming a team, I would discover, is almost genetic. Every team goes through the same process, or at least parts of the process until they either gel or crumble. Our team would be no exception to the rule.

At our first meeting, everyone came prepared with his or her drawings and ideas. The first stage of team development, as I have been told, is **testing**. During this phase, everyone is tenuous about their position in the group, very evasive, lacking in real honesty, and like anyone's experience in elementary school, afraid to raise their hand and ask a question.

We went around the table as each chef presented what they wanted to prepare in Germany. To a person, the response from the group was always positive. "Looks great. Terrific idea. Great plate design." As we started to become comfortable with select members of the team, we carried on side conversations that were far more honest.

"Can you believe he wants to make that for an Olympic competition?"

"That's really crap, I can't believe he thinks that is worthy of this caliber competition."

Roland thanked everyone for coming and said that our next meeting would be an opportunity to more closely define what each of us would be making, building on that day's presentation. That meeting would follow the format of the first.

While the team (I use the term loosely) was trying to develop a game plan, many friends were building a campaign to raise the necessary funds to get us to Germany. As it would turn out, those funds approached $250,000. Fortunately, the team did not have to spend much time on this; there were many other dedicated individuals who did a fantastic job in this regard.

At a later meeting we were informed that the team would be presenting a table for judging at the upcoming Boston Restaurant Show in April. The Northeast Food Service and Lodging Show would be flying in judges from Germany, and the Press would be all over us. The sponsors that had already signed on would be standing by to take pride in their investment in our team.

We arrived at the Boston University kitchen to prepare for the show. Most of us brought partially prepared items that WE had independently designed and spent two days putting the finishing touches on, making our sauces and glazing everything in multiple layers of aspic. Ten chefs, apprentices and team assistants packed the kitchen as we all went on our individual missions towards completion of platters, plates and centerpieces.

We were to be at the show by 6 a.m. to set-up, as the judges would be arriving promptly at 8. The kitchen was in total chaos. Every pot and pan was dirty, aspic was everywhere, and organization was far from the flavor of the day. I was one of the first ones to arrive at the show at 8:30. The judges were waiting. It would be over an hour before we were finally set, at least as set as we could be.

After judging, the team members were awarded one silver and two bronze medals. This presentation was hardly a stellar performance and a true embarrassment to all involved. At the end, we packed up our equipment, paid some BU cleaners to take care of the disaster in the kitchen, and went our separate ways. I was sure that our team and the quest for the Olympics were over.

A few weeks later I had another call from Tony Flory stating that we were to have another team meeting soon, location to be determined. I offered the college as a site and he gladly accepted.

A Turning Point in Team Development

We were very excited at Paul Smith's. Students were anticipating the opportunity to prepare meals for the team, kitchens were ready, local restaurants were prepared for various recognition dinners, the mayor of Lake Placid was prepared to give the team members a key to the Olympic Village, and a new president at Paul Smith's had no idea what was going on.

The team arrived, a tour of the facilities ensued, and a meeting was called in a second floor classroom. Now, the second phase of team development is referred to as **infighting**. During this phase there is a struggle for place, a definition of power within the group, and an indication of whether a team will solidify or break apart.

Later on students told me they felt a need to leave the building. The arguments were so intense and colorful with language they were nervous about being so close to the action. For the first time since we were formed, the team was honest, brutally honest. No longer did people brush over the issues at hand. Some team members were told that the products they had chosen to make were not their forte. Others were told that to select an item or theme without a team strategy was absurd. One team member had conflicts with his new job and had been unable to make previous meetings or even the competition in Boston. We decided it was in the best interest of the team to ask him to withdraw.

In the end, once everything was on the table, we started to talk about each other's strengths. With this in mind, we quickly went from the second phase of team development to the third, **organization**. We defined what each player would do as part of a cohesive effort. This is how it went.

Every team member was categorized as either a hot food presented cold, cold platter, or pastry chef. Some were assigned centerpieces for various presentations and everyone was given an additional assignment that was indicative of their real team strength.

Joe (Jose') was/is the most phenomenal vegetable carver I have ever seen. Nearly everyone had some type of intricate vegetable carving on their program so it was decided that Joe would either assist with or complete the carvings for each team member. Roland had a keen eye for plate and platter layouts. It then became his role to assist with the design of plates and platters. Danny has many talents, but one in particular focused on centerpieces made from salt dough. This simple air-dry dough formula could be used to shape and sculpt incredible centerpieces that were subsequently painted with burnt cornstarch and dark rum. The end result was incredible. Danny would be one of our feature sculptors to set the theme for table presentations in Germany. Mickey, the good humor man and glue that held the team together, was a master at glazing food with aspic. He dedicated himself the becoming the aspic scientist and defined how each member would finish their food for presentation. Walter was a major part of the team's creative energy. He saw things differently and forced all of us to put on our innovation hats when it came to determining what we would produce. Finally, I was given the task of helping to organize everyone's program. Recipes, drawings, production sheets, etc. would be developed into book form that would be at the chef's disposal through production.

On the pastry side, there could not be a more focused group of professionals working together and complementing each other. Lars was the seasoned veteran and became everyone's most trusted critic. He was awesome at sugar work. George was certainly close in terms of skills, but had a unique ability to help everyone keep the whole process in perspective. Neil was a master at working with chocolate and became the team resource for this medium. He also took it upon himself to get the team looking good through sponsorship of uniforms, jackets, etc.

Finally, things were coming together. We continued our time at Paul Smith's with the first real presentation of product for critique. Three of us presented while the others assisted. This would be our format from that point on. Every program would be everyone's responsibility.

I was one of the chefs to present, since it was my home turf. Tony Flory brought a fellow chef, Dieter, to help with the critique. I invited the new college president down for the critique so that he could gain some perspective on the process. After we were done he pulled me aside and said that if we critiqued faculty with that much intensity, we would lose them all. Honesty was the call to arms from this point on.

Roland decided that we would begin meeting every other week and each time the chefs would present for critique. It was stated that although a real theme would not be developed, the premise of our program would evolve around indigenous New England ingredients.

It was June, and we would be leaving for Germany in October. A considerable amount of work was ahead of us if we were to save face and not embarrass our sponsors.

Over the next 4 months, I put over 7,000 miles on my car traveling back and forth to Boston for practices. We researched, developed, improved, changed, and evolved over the last phase of our preparations. One of the best decisions we made was a replacement for our displaced team member. Through the recommendations of Danny and Roland, we brought Charles (Chuck) on as the youngest member of our group. In his early twenties, Chuck was very talented, a bit cocky, but ready, willing and quite able to fill the void. The team was complete in many ways.

In October we assembled in Boston for packing and discussions about our final strategy. I had spent three days and nights prior to my arrival in Boston completing advance preparations in Paul Smith's kitchens with the assistance of some terrific student apprentices. At this level of competition, everything had to be perfect. When I called for a brunoise of carrots, each carrot had to be a perfect 1/8-inch cube, measured!

We learned a few tricks along the way. It was much easier to prepare major items like galantines, terrines and pates in the States and transport them over to Germany, but they could not be frozen and we were very concerned about maintaining freshness. An alternative form of preservation was devised: we immersed the completed items in tubs of warm aspic and allowed them to set. The aspic kept air away from the pieces and extended their shelf life in the same manner than cryovac would. Additionally, we would just re-melt the aspic for glazing later on.

The centerpieces had been completed and would be packaged like Rodin sculptures from Musee D'Orsay in Paris. Massive plywood transportation boxes with styrofoam and foam rubber were designed to protect incredible salt dough pieces that were over four feet high. Danny made two amazing pieces. One salt dough piece was a model of the earth topped by an American eagle with spread wings; the other was a horse in full gallop, mounted by an American Indian in full headdress. Others with North American Geese and Ducks were created by Roland and Jose'. My salt dough piece was much smaller, depicting the bounty of American produce.

Neil prepared an incredible chocolate centerpiece that was a bust of an American Indian, again in full headdress. This piece was so delicate that we did not want to put it in storage on the plane, so we bought an extra ticket for the centerpiece and strapped it in a seat. The joke was who would get the Indian's meal. Finally, George and Lars had sugar pieces and a marzipan mantle clock.

All in all we had over 1 ton of equipment and food to transport in addition to the ten-team members, advisors, apprentices and spouses—thirty people (thirty-one including the chocolate Indian) in all and a cargo box full of necessities. We boarded the Lufthansa plane en route for Frankfurt.

The demeanor of the team was dramatically improved from our dreadful performance in April. We were nervous, but unified. Our goal was to do the best we could and not embarrass all those people who had helped us get to this point.

Those people included chefs of New England, Dole and Bailey Purveyors of Boston, The Epicurean Club of Boston, The New England Chapters of the American Culinary Federation, F. Dick Knives, and a plethora of others too numerous to mention, but never forgotten.

Arriving in Frankfurt, there were hundreds of chefs from all over the world moving through German customs. When customs saw us in our team jackets, they just waived us through. Tony and Roland, both having been born in Austria, had paved the way for us and it appeared that this was part of their work.

We moved into the pension where we would be staying for a week and toured our kitchen in an insurance building in downtown Frankfurt. We drove the route from the kitchen to the Misen Gladen (convention center) where the Olympics were to be held. Now it suddenly hit home; we would be representing the United States at the most prestigious culinary competition in the world.

Michael Minor and Minor Foods sponsored the area where we would present. Minor is the premier food base company in the United States and Michael is a chef who is a true friend to all other chefs. His contribution to our involvement in the Olympics was incredible.

We would be sharing the kitchen with the Austrian National Team with their five chefs, apprentices and advisors. In total, there would be nearly twenty cooks in the same facility at any time. The kitchen was used each day from 6 a.m. until 2 p.m. After that it was exclusively ours. We could still use some of the space on a limited basis during the morning, but nothing too extensive.

We would be working, on average, 20 hours per day, for the next eight days. We unpacked all of our food, set-up a refrigerated truck in the parking lot as our storage, checked the integrity of everything that had just flown 4,000 miles and got together for the only formal dinner we would have together for more than a week. Amazingly, everything made the trip in good shape. A few minor repairs to the salt dough pieces were needed, but other than that we were in good shape.

The first day of production in the kitchen was interrupted by a call from German customs. Tony and Roland had to pay them a visit, immediately. Shortly thereafter, we received a frantic call from Roland.

"Customs is on their way. Apparently, we were not allowed to bring any turkey or pork from New England into Europe, and since this was the mainstay of our program, we are facing a huge problem. They want to take everything away and destroy it. Hide all the critical things and make sure they find something that we don't need that they can actually destroy!" We had to stop what we were doing and scramble to adjust to this twist of fate. What we didn't know was that Roland and Tony could have been arrested for what we brought into the country.

As it turned out, thanks to their Austrian background and diplomacy we worked out a deal. The team assured customs that nothing we produced was for consumption and that we would throw it out immediately after each day of the competition. They would send a customs officer to our table at the end of each day to insure that we did just that.

The first two days were just production. The show would not begin until day three. This gave everyone a chance to get ahead. The plan of attack was simple: each day of the five-day competition, two of our chefs would display on our expansive 24-foot buffet table. Centerpieces would be presented each day and would accumulate until on the final day, all salt dough pieces would be shown. On the date before each chef's show day, everyone else except the two who would display the following day were assigned to help. Thus, the show chefs had six other potential apprentices.

Let me explain the concept of the Olympic competition. There are two parts to the competition: cold food and hot food. The cold competition featured pastry, cold buffet platters and hot food/presented cold (for the eye). None of these foods were tasted, only critiqued based on visual presentation. Now you might ask, how can you judge food without tasting it? The judges are professional chefs, and chefs can envision flavor by looking at how ingredients are used, the spices and herbs that are present, and the quality of workmanship. The second part of the competition was reserved only for national teams. Each member country of the World Association of Cooks Society (WACS) presents one national team. This group of chefs competes in the cold portion of the show and the hot food competition where food is presented for judges and public tasting. Our team was allowed to compete in only the cold portion.

The United States also hosted 18 Regional Teams such as ours in 1988. The number of Regional Teams from around the world was over 60 and with individual competitors, the total number of chefs competing well exceeded 1,000.

Back to our kitchen, the first two chefs who would represent us were Danny and Mickey. These two were selected because of how well they were organized, but also because their assistance with everyone else was critical. We worked all night helping them finish their programs. At around four a.m. we packed the van with custom made storage shelving and began the trip to the show at around ten miles per hour (to avoid any sudden jarring of the food platters). It would take approximately two hours to set-up the table; touch up the food (the show chefs would walk around with painter's detail brushes, touching up with hot aspic). When they were set, the rest of us would go back to the Pension for two hours of sleep, a quick breakfast, and then back to the kitchen. The show chefs would stay with the table until after judging, as would Tony, our team manager.

In the kitchen we took a break for a meal. Everyone was pretty quiet, due to nerves and an acute lack of sleep. The phone rang and Roland got up to answer it. He returned to the table and sat down next to me. He turned and asked, very calmly, "What would be better than a gold medal?"

My response to Roland's question was "Nothing".

He then said, "How about two perfect scores!" Danny and Mickey had both received gold medals and one of them with special merit (only a handful received this recognition during the competition). The surge of adrenaline in the room was apparent as we all beamed with tremendous pride. Never in our wildest dreams did we expect this.

Danny and Mickey's success became our inspiration. Over the next five days of competition, every team member received a gold medal for their work and five had perfect scores.

The last day of the show, the German Chefs Association and WACS awarded the actual medals. We arrived at the grand hall in the Misen Gladen. It was filled with thousands of people in white chefs' coats and toques. The parade of flags from each country was reminiscent of the sporting Olympics. When the bagpipers from Scotland arrived and their instruments reverberated through the hall, a rush of pride was evident in all of us.

I remember the nervousness when they called my name and I walked up the stairs to the stage to receive a gold medal from the greatest culinary event in the world. It was very hard to fight off the tears. In the final moments, additional awards were given. All the regional teams were brought up to the stage and they announced the grand prize for the best regional team in the world. We won this designation and were quickly referred to as the Cinderella Team. Nineteen gold medals and the grand prize. Not bad for a team that almost fell apart six months earlier.

There were some tense moments through the competition, but overall we had fun. We came with cautious optimism and a realization that the fact that we gelled as a team was as important as how we did in the battle for medals. In the end, we exceeded everyone's expectations, including our own.

Lesson to all: Teams are where it's at!

The team was elated, but thoroughly exhausted. Our spouses had seen a great deal of Germany; we had only seen the kitchen. Now it was time to celebrate and we only wanted to sleep. Michael Minor took care of this. He rented an entire old-world restaurant in the Saxon House District of Frankfurt for the American chefs. Saxon House was the only part of Frankfurt that was not destroyed during WWII. The restaurant was right out of the story books (by the way, I fell asleep in the cab ride on the way to the restaurant). The women servers were dressed in traditional clothes and carried tankards of German beer (six at a time) to every table. Platters of food including sausages, smoked pigs' knuckles, sauerkraut and mashed potatoes, were brought to all of us (each was large enough to serve three people) and Michael Minor toasted the greatest chefs in the world. It was a moment that I will never forget.

The next day, the team left for Austria. We enjoyed a couple days of vacation before returning home. We drove all night in a tour bus on the Autobahn at speeds that are hard to imagine. What we did not realize was that the team was out of money. We were headed to Austria, broke. On the bus with us was one of our key supporters, cheerleader, and sponsor-Bud Matteson, the owner of Dole and Bailey. Without any fanfare, Bud took care of the team's vacation so that we could celebrate our accomplishments. He was like our team father.

In Austria, we were the guests of the Austrian National Team who'd shared the kitchen with us in Frankfurt. We stayed in a pension operated by one of the Austrian team members. We had a few drinks and went to bed, having arrived late at night. The next morning we woke up and looked outside, suddenly realizing that we were surrounded by the Alps. The view was breathtaking, right out of the Sound of Music. This was Innsbruck, home to the Olympic games, sister to Lake Placid. We received the key to the city from the mayor and spent the day as tourists through this magnificent haven in the old world portion of Europe.

That night we were guests at a family restaurant owned by another chef from the Austrian team. We traveled by bus deep into the forests of Austria until we arrived at a Hansel and Gretelish property that no one but real locals could ever find again. When we walked in, we realized that the restaurant was ours for the evening. There were some guests of local flavor including the owner of Szworsky Crystal, the world famous producer of those magnificent crystal figurines.

The Austrians love schnapps. We began with a toast of schnapps to chefs everywhere and throughout the night we toasted to just about anything and everything (we were quickly over-served). At a point in the evening, the host chef took our team and the Austrian team into his private wine cellar, where only family had ever been before. We sat around an oak table and drank wines from his private collection, toasting our newly acquired friendship. I can't remember exactly what we toasted, but I am sure it was close to being blood brothers for life.

Coming home was almost a disappointment. We arrived in Logan Airport, collected our belongings, shook hands and hugged and went back to our normal lives.

Arriving back at Paul Smith's, I was embarrassed by how well I was received. The faculty had arranged to cancel classes that first day so that students, faculty, administrators and friends could help to celebrate the team's accomplishments. I was given a special recognition from the State Legislature, an honorary gold medal from the Lake Placid Olympic Committee, and an honorary title from the president of the college as "chef extraordinaire." The greatest recognition was a standing ovation from my students, especially those who had helped as apprentices during preparation for the competition.

Life lesson: Our greatest accomplishments in life are not measured by what we do, but by the people whom we meet and the friendships we create.

Friends for Life

What is the definition of a true friend? Is he/she a person who would lay their life down for you, or is that just a fable? Is he/she a person who will be there for you whenever you need them? Yes! How many of us can say that they have true friends like this? Hopefully, you have at least one. I now had nine friends of this caliber—add this to Rick, my all-time best friend, and I felt very fortunate.

Through the years, to this day, I know that I can always count on these guys. We talk a few times a year, most of us, and feel very comfortable asking each other for advice or favors. We are always honest with each other.

Please note: Once a true team, always a true team. The three musketeers had nothing on us.

We have met for formal and informal reunions in Boston, Lake Placid, Paul Smith's, Chicago, New York, and even Las Vegas. My calendar is always open for the next gathering of the team.

4

Building a Program's Image

What many traditional educators refuse to recognize is that higher education today is a business, a very serious business. No different than running a hotel or restaurant where the first objective is to fill the seats with customers, colleges need to fill the chairs with students. Some feel that this is blasphemy, yet it is absolutely true. Our customer is the student. This does not imply we are to give anything away; students still need to earn their grades and their diploma, but they are consumers who are spending extravagant amounts of money for a product and a service. There are numerous competing schools that are more than willing to take those students off your hands if you fail to recognize your role as business people.

In the arena of culinary arts, there are more than 700 (best guess) colleges offering programs. Many of them are actually doing a terrific job. As a program director, it was my job to figure out ways to make the college attractive as, if not more attractive than much of the competition. This is not an easy task when your school is located in the middle of the Adirondacks, where winters are long and very hard.

Paul Smith's began its culinary program in 1980. The field was already packed with solid competitors with a great deal of name recognition. The Culinary Institute of America, Johnson and Wales, California Culinary and numerous others had already defined their position in the marketplace. Paul Smith's is located in a very rural area, difficult to market location, particularly as it pertains to an industry that is typically urban.

I remember back to the days of my youth when I watched those great TV shows like Gunsmoke, The Rifleman, and Wagon Train or even those terrific spaghetti westerns that featured the up-and-coming Clint Eastwood. When a small group of bandits wanted to fool the posse into thinking they were bigger and more dangerous than reality, they would run between rocks and trees, fire their guns and move on to others and do the same. This gave the perception of might and the threat of serious competitiveness. This was my strategy. If you aren't big, make people think that you are.

Remember, I am a cook, not a marketer, but I found the challenge to be quite invigorating. Fortunately, the college, at the time, was willing to support the process. I began by making contacts with key industry people and organizations, joining, and becoming involved in their activities. I joined the American Culinary Federation and established an Adirondack Chapter, I joined the National Restaurant Association and participated in their workshops, I joined the New York State Restaurant Association and participated in their annual show. I ordered a professional booth display and rented booth space at the Northeast Foodservice Show in Boston, the National Restaurant Show in Chicago, and the American Culinary Federation Convention, adding to our established presence at the New York Hotel Show. Wherever the big players were located, we were there. When people saw the CIA or J and W, they also saw Paul Smith's.

Our student culinary team was designed to be very serious and competed each year in Boston at the Northeast Show and I made sure that I also competed there and in New York at the Society Culinaire Philanthropique Salon. It was just like the spaghetti westerns, moving from rock to rock, making everyone feel that we were bigger than we were.

Whether a result of this strategy or simple reflex to a growing need for cooks and an increase in the prestige of the position, the culinary program began to grow from 23 students to nearly 300 by 2002.

THE AMERICAN CULINARY FEDERATION

I joined the American Culinary Federation (ACF) in 1980, forming a local Adirondack chapter in the same year. Since this was the most respected national organization of chefs in the United States, I was certain that involvement in the Federation would be crucial to the success of the Culinary Program at Paul Smith's.

In those days, the ACF was really coming of age. The organization had existed since the nineteen twenties, but in 1980 being a member of the ACF meant that you were part of a movement. Chefs were now professionals, people with admirable skills in a profession that was growing in popularity. The ACF had all the potential of becoming the beacon of light for all who sought to spend a good portion of their lives cooking for others.

The ACF had, since 1976, taken the lead in defining what it would mean to be a chef. They were the only organization with a formalized certification process of cooks and chefs, the only organization recognized by the Department of Labor for their cook apprenticeship program, had sponsored successful Culinary Olympic Teams, and were successful in changing the official status of the cook from domestic to professional in the eyes of the U.S. Government.

I wanted Paul Smith's to be a part of this movement. My assumption was that area cooks and chefs would also share my enthusiasm to learn, collaborate, communicate and improve. Paul Smith's did and has continued to be involved with the ACF, but my assumption about other local chefs proved incorrect.

I am not bashing local chefs, there were many reasons why the local chapter did not work, as I am sure other chapters have discovered over the years. Typical chefs with 70 plus hour work weeks have little time to invest in discussions about their profession outside of their restaurant. The ACF, as it grew, became less of a vehicle for chefs to share and improve, and more political and bureaucratic as it grew from a few thousand members to over 20,000 with multiple chapters in every state.

After thirteen years, our local chapter was mothballed, with no scheduled meetings since 1994. Even during our peak of activity, it was difficult to attract more than a dozen members to a meeting.

In 1990, I applied for accreditation by the American Culinary Federation's Educational Institute (ACFEI) and after completing the comprehensive Self-Study and a subsequent site visit by a team of ACF Chefs, was granted a five-year initial accreditation. This was very beneficial because it gave us all a sense of pride in the validation of what we were doing and a means of establishing a level of differentiation from many of our competitors. Additionally, students who graduated from the program would be allowed to apply for the first level of certification, Certified Cook.

My personal involvement in the ACF grew exponentially when Mary Peterson, Director, asked me to serve on the Accrediting Commission of the ACF. My four-year tenure with the Commission would eventually lead to the position of Chairman of the ACFEI, a two-year appointment with an additional year as past Chairman.

The President of the ACF, during my time as Chair of the ACFEI was Noel Cullen, a Certified Master Chef and Ph.D. who taught at Boston University. Noel was an accomplished chef, Olympic Competitor, Culinary Team Captain and Manager, and author. Noel, although sometimes controversial, was intent on bring the ACF to another level of notoriety, respect and service to its membership.

The ACFEI was dissolved as a separate entity and reformed as the Education Services Committee of the ACF during my first year as Chairman. We added Access ACF as a new service that focused on validation of high school culinary programs, modified the levels and process for chef certification, and streamlined the Accreditation process as well. I had an opportunity to serve with some exceptional individuals who were dedicated to education and to the culinary arts and became very aware of the issues and inter-workings of the ACF.

I believe the greatest strength and greatest weakness of the ACF stems from the fact that it is a federation and not an association. As a federation, the organization is a cluster of more than 300 chapters of chefs, who although they adhere to many of the standards that the federation espouses, work to a large degree by their own set of goals and objectives. Each chapter is also entitled to express their thoughts on how the organization should be run, and do so through frequent election of officers at the regional and national level. This has a tendency to create too much formality and bureaucracy at the chapter level, and in my opinion, keeps young new cooks and chefs from joining. Without this "new blood," this potentially wonderful organization will face some tough times in the future.

Great service organizations are designed to respond quickly to client needs and to innovate very quickly as the business environment they are in changes. The ACF, in the past decade, has lost some innovative ground to other interesting organizations such as the Research Chefs Association (RCA), International Association of Cooking Professionals (IACP), Women Chefs and Restaurateurs (WCR), Retail Bakers Association (RBA), The National Restaurant Association (NRA), and the American Dietetic Association (ADA).

If the ACF were an Association, such as the NRA and ADA, they could be more responsive, minimize the combative infighting that inevitably exists in a grouping of so many chapters, and reach for a higher level of influence in the culinary community. The ACF could and should be the true "authority on food" in the United States, as they so proclaim. It is a shame, for instance, that the ACF is not often consulted by government organizations and the press on food issues and they have little to no exposure on the Food Network.

As another example, certification is a fantastic process that should have more meaning in American culinary circles. A strong fundamental knowledge of preparation, food safety, management, and professionalism is absolutely critical in today's kitchens. Just as hospitals are required to hire registered dietitians and nurses, so too should all restaurants be required to hire a certified cook or chef. This would lend trust and confidence to the millions of patrons who place their health and well-being in the hands of cooks every day. Yet aside from the personal gratification of meeting the criteria and passing the testing involved, there is little benefit to the culinarian who seeks certification and very little understanding and recognition on the part of the restaurant patron.

In 1996, Paul Smith's applied for re-accreditation by the ACF and after another Self-Study and site visit was awarded a seven-year accreditation and then again in 2003. Of the 700 culinary schools in the country, less than 20% are accredited. This continued to place Paul Smith's in a cluster of elite schools that met these exacting criteria.

THE VALUE OF A CULINARY EDUCATION

Do we really need degree programs in cooking and will this level of education help to create better chefs? This, of course, is a terrific question.

I think that it is important to make some distinctions first. cooks and chefs are different in many respects. First, there is little question that the ideal way to learn how to cook is on-the-job, in a professional kitchen. Without the pressures of day-to-day production and the presence of a customer, many aspects of becoming a professional cook will be absent in a student's education. The key words here are "professional kitchen." Although the food industry is massive and growing every day, there are still many kitchens that fall short of the professional classification. There are even fewer that invest in development of new ideas and products, and still fewer that understand the significance of what they do. Most good chefs are trainers, but this does not necessarily mean that they are teachers. A teacher is patient, well versed, and current in their knowledge, and understanding of the various levels of learning that individual's function at.

So theoretically, the best environment to learn how to cook is in a production kitchen, realistically, most kitchens are not prepared to teach.

Second, a chef is a different animal than a cook. Andre Soltner once said to an audience of chefs, "Let us not forget that we are all cooks." This is certainly true; all chefs must continue to appreciate being cooks, but not all cooks can appreciate what it means to be a chef. A chef today is a manager of people, product, finances, and image. He or she will spend a disproportionate part of their day dealing with the administration of these functions and only a small portion of time with the actual process of cooking.

A degree program in culinary arts should then provide far greater breadth of learning than simply to focus on cooking skills. The foundations of cuisine must be strong, but are best enhanced through application in a real environment. An education should also help young people to become cognizant of the needs of people, worldly enough to understand that everything impacts on a restaurant's success, confident enough to make decisions, intelligent enough to assimilate information and analyze it effectively, and strong enough to come to a conclusion that is in the best interest of the majority even when the vocal minority is on the other side of the fence. This is what it means to be a chef.

Management is a Bittersweet Job

To be perfectly honest, most of the time it sucks to be a manager. Some of you may disagree, but when you have been in that position for quite some time you will realize that although the most fruitful career tracks focus on being a manager, individuals in those roles lose more than they gain. Here are some reality pills that are hard to swallow:

- Managers cannot be friends with their employees. They can be friendly and caring, but not friends. Why, you may ask? Because it is very difficult to make a decision, even the right one, if it may negatively impact on a friendship.

- No matter what decision you make, there will be some who agree, some who disagree, and some who will hate you for making it.

- Managers have to worry about everyone's performance, not just their own.

- Ultimately, everything that happens is the direct or indirect responsibility of the manager.

- Most employees, in just about any industry believe that they could manage better than you.

- In some cases, they are right.

- If you entered this business to cook, remember that executive chefs rarely get to enjoy that aspect of the field, they are managers first.

- Most cooks who become chef/managers still have those fragile artist egos that are very easily bruised. Ninety-nine happy customers are spoiled by one who is not.

- Even though you may not have cooked their meal, you hired, trained, coached and directed the person who did. If the meal is wrong, it's your fault.

Culinary programs are designed to produce chefs. At least that is what they should be doing because no one should spend $40-$80,000 to learn how to become a cook. A person would never be able to pay back that debt on a cook's salary. Good, bad or indifferent, once you commit to a college education, the chef's position should be in your sights.

There are some things that a college education can never prepare the student for. The broken record mantra of all educators is "You will work many, many hours as a chef." Unfortunately, students never fully believe you. I can't tell you how many times an alumnus said, "I never realized how hard I would be working." Duh? Every chef instructor I know, whether at Paul Smith's or any other institution has repeatedly said, "a 60–75 hour work week is the norm, six or seven days per week (eight if we could figure out a way to stretch a work week), including holidays, and never expect to be home before nine or ten in the evening." Still, they don't believe it. Get this: It is worse than we told you!

Another thing that colleges are unable to teach is the intensity of the kitchen moment. How do you keep your composure and sense of quality when the board is filled with 30 dupes, the expeditor is barking out another handful of orders, the heat by the battery of ranges is about 140 degrees, sweat is raining off your forehead, you have so many burns on your hands that it is laughable, you are running out of mise en place and there are still three hours of service left, and half of your staff doesn't even speak English. The protected days of cooking in a lab with ample time to do things right seems so far in the past and so unrealistic.

It is, however, those days of methodical training that will keep you from sacrificing the commitment to quality that all schools strive to embed in a student's mind.

This brings up a story that I constantly use in my classes about a friend of mine who was a maitre d'. I was paying him a visit one afternoon about an hour before they opened for service. I noticed his servers measuring the distance from the edge of the silverware to the edge of the table, lining up glassware with a straight edge, steaming and polishing wine glasses, and spacing chairs evenly from the front and sides of each table. I was amazed. When I asked him why he would ever go to this extreme, his reply became imbedded in my sub-conscious: "I strive for 100% perfection before service to set a benchmark in employees' minds. I know that when we are working at our peak of business, service will slip. This is inevitable. The glassware won't be perfect, the silver won't be exact, and chairs may be a bit off-center. If, however, my service staff understands perfection, they won't let it slip too much. We may be at 90%, but that will still be heads above our competition."

Finally, colleges can't teach the reality of managing other people. I have always tried to believe that people are inherently good, hard working, dedicated, and anxious to strive for excellence. This is what we all should believe and certainly what must be taught in school. Once in the industry, the following reality smacks you in the face: Not everyone is hard-working, many are lazy by choice; many employees in the restaurant business are not dedicated because they would rather be doing something else, and at times it seems like the majority of people have no desire to strive for excellence—mediocrity is just fine. With all this in mind, eager culinarians on the way to chefdom are in for a surprise.

It would be very easy to simply say: "Hire the right people ." I have used this phrase myself, many times. Unfortunately, just like you can't choose your family members, you can't always choose the employees that you inherit. Getting a good day's work out of them becomes your life goal. Reasonable quality starts to take over for pursuit of excellence in far too many food service establishments. Don't believe me? Then obviously you have not worked in enough operations yet.

Years ago I read, with a bit of anger, an article by Andy Rooney (who I still can't tolerate). In the article he made a very bold statement: "In France it is nearly impossible to find a bad restaurant and in America it is nearly impossible to find a good one." I was irate. I fired off a response and sent it to every known trade periodical in the country stating how ignorant he was and that he had insulted thousands of proud chefs and restaurateurs in one of the largest industries in the United States. The letter was printed in Nations Restaurant News, Restaurants and Institutions, and Restaurants U.S.A. I never did receive a letter of apology from Andy Rooney.

That letter was sent about 15 years ago. Since then I have traveled to many parts of this country and have been overseas on eight different occasions. My conclusion, although it is beginning to change: he wasn't too far off the mark. The problem is a work force half of which is increasingly difficult to motivate and the other half is comprised of a cluster of quality food service professionals who are burned out.

You will work very hard and many, many hours. Ok, I get it, but why? How can we really expect young people not to challenge this absurd un-written rule of becoming a chef or restaurateur? I am not a bleeding heart. I worked those hours (and still do), and often actually enjoyed it, but there comes a time when enough is enough. There is nothing wrong with a 50-hour workweek and two days off. This is part of the grand design. Even God had a day of rest.

5

Decisions Don't Come Easy in a College Environment

From the outside looking in, one would think that colleges are on the cutting edge of what is happening and thus able to respond quickly to industry and student needs. Nothing could be further from the truth. There is probably no greater example of a dysfunctional democracy than education. Remember the definition of a democracy as a government of the people, by the people, and for the people? Well, this is the intent of democracy, but realistically that does not always work. This is why we elect representatives to make those decisions for us. If we don't like their decision-making history, then we make a change during the next election (that is if we actually show up to vote). The problem with a true democracy is that it is too slow. In a fast-changing world, slow responses can spell disaster.

Apply this to education and you will see one of the last bastions of hope for a true democracy. We live for committees and meetings, we cower at the directives from outside agencies who are old in their thinking, and we spend most of our time figuring out ways to protect what we have and avoid inevitable change.

Those colleges that try to approach education differently, that are innovative and responsive, are oftentimes shunned by their peers, regardless of any success they may have with their initiatives.

If any other business were to operate like education, they would shutter their doors before they even knew what hit them.

Everything that you read today about the state of business, the demands of a customer-driven economy, the intensity of competition, points towards "real-time response" on the part of successful organizations. An issue arises; a need develops, a change is anticipated, the company responds, NOW!

Education has always been different, so obviously it will remain so. At least that is what many who live within the framework of education truly believe. Here are some personal observations and totally un-scientific predictions:

- Education is on the verge of world-class change.
  Unfortunately, most educators and educational systems have blinders on and will not survive the purge.

- Education is pricing itself out of the market and with little to no way of guaranteeing outcomes; this level of expenditure will be seriously questioned by the marketplace.

- Formal degrees will begin to mean less as a few radical education players are able to actually guarantee results through new methods of teaching and training. These methods may not result in a degree.

- Some very successful businesses will begin to develop their own educational vehicles that are cost-effective, focused, and results oriented.

- Value will become the "call to arms" in the process of selecting a means of educating the masses. Those institutions that cannot provide value for the money spent will not survive.

- The college experience will dramatically evolve, as a discerning population of consumers will no longer tolerate typical "unquestioned" conditions. Residence hall life will be replaced by hotel-like environments and services; cafeterias will cease to exist and will be replaced by multiple dining options; technology at the most current level of excellence will be a price of admission, and real-time asynchronous curriculum delivery will be a part of every educational program. Finally, mass-customization in curriculum development will be just as powerful in colleges as the concept is in manufacturing.

The problem is that most colleges have no grasp of the changes about to occur. They are creatures of history, bogged down in bureaucratic mud, sinking deeper every day, without any desire to reach for a lifeline and pull themselves out.

As an example, the fastest-growing providers of culinary education in America today are a small faction of highly aggressive and very effective proprietary schools. These schools define a need and act; determine a prime location, and build; find the right talent, and hire them; determine a potential market for students, and inundate that market with pro-active advertising. This is beyond the comprehension of typical colleges, but commonplace in most other businesses.

Culinary Colleges need to begin to think differently. At the same time, the food service industry needs to become far more pro-active in defining what it is that they are looking for in young culinarians.

Most of the material that leads to a level of professional competence cannot be defined within the parameters of a course. As an example, if a restaurant owner were to ask one very significant question of a culinarian applying for the position of chef, it would be: "What can you bring to the table to help us become successful?" This is, the real question—isn't it?

"I have great taste buds and can make the best corn chowder you have ever eaten," is not enough anymore. A serious look at the position requires candidates to be worldly, appreciative and knowledgeable about other cultures, well read, articulate both orally and in written form, intuitive, creative, pleasant but firm as a manager, cost conscious, a judge of great talent, interesting, professional looking, very well organized, and a great cook, of course.

Shouldn't a culinary program help to prepare a young student for these characteristics of a successful chef? Put another way, how many truly great chefs are working in restaurants today without possessing most if not all of those traits? I would dare say, almost none.

Any solid culinary program must then be methodically designed to train good cooks, create knowledgeable and interesting people, prepare individuals to be solid business persons, and demonstrate to those individuals how to look and act like the professionals that they hope to become. Can this be done through a series of courses, or should it be done through an integrated curriculum that allows individuals to practice all of these characteristics or competencies on an ongoing basis? Obviously, you see where I am going.

Many industry recruiters seek out individuals with a real talent for preparing and presenting food, but what they really want, in the long run, are individuals who have a much greater breadth of skills and aptitudes. Too many schools spend the lion's share of time in their curricula, preparing better cooks instead of preparing individuals to be chefs, managers and leaders.

This is what the food service industry should promote, this is what the best colleges should provide, and this is what serious culinarians should consider when preparing to spend an enormous amount of money on a college education. If they simply want to become a better cook, then seek out one of the excellent apprenticeship programs in the United States and save the money.

This is really what it comes down to. How come the chicken isn't getting brown is an effect of a much greater cause. Colleges are businesses, but will only remain businesses if they produce and guarantee positive results. Businesses that do not select, profile, serve, and evaluate their customers, threaten their own futures. How come the chicken isn't getting brown is not a culinary question; it is a question of a student's ability to analyze a situation and make a logical decision. It is the consummate question that defines a student customer's ability to succeed, and a college's focus on meeting the real objectives of an education.

The question was comical at first and disheartening in the short-term, but enlightening in the long run. This one question defined, for me at least, what a culinary education and career in food service is all about.

A course in soups does not make a student a great preparer of soups. It is an understanding of culture, the nature of the ingredients, the history of the methods used in preparing soups and a lot of practice that makes a great soup cook.

A course in English composition will not prepare a person to be a solid written communicator. Life experiences, understanding human behavior, interactions with people, constant reading and lots of practice will make solid writers.

I have no scientific analytical data to support this hypothesis, but I know I am right. This might be a very presumptuous statement, yet I believe that you could go to the bank with it. Colleges that do not challenge the old methods of delivering content and begin to focus on ways to achieve results will fade away. Culinary institutions that do not realize that their job is to prepare individuals to be more than good cooks are ignoring the value formula and will be in line for a very sudden and frightening wake-up call.

In America we believe that everyone should have the right to choose what he or she wants to do with his or her life and pursue that dream with reckless abandon. Of course, this sounds great, but the assumption is that everyone has the aptitude and the right attitude to be successful in any venture that they choose.

Cooking is not innate. We are not born cooks; we are trained to be cooks. The job is demanding and just like any other trade, developing the necessary skills to be successful takes tremendous discipline and a willingness to put the time in. Yes, there is the issue of dexterity and stamina, but aside from that it all boils down to attitude. If a student of culinary arts truly loves food, I mean really loves food, and everything about it; then they have a chance to be successful. Here is a simple test that will help any wannabe chef make the right decision:

CULINARY ATTITUDE SELF-TEST
(Check all that you agree with whole-heatedly)

- I would rather cook than anything else.

- I don't mind working in kitchens where the average temperature is above 100 degrees.

- I have the stamina to work on my feet for 10–12 hours per day, 6 days per week.

- I currently have a cookbook collection and whenever someone asks me for gift ideas, I say "cookbooks".

- Whenever I visit another town or city, I always research what great restaurants grace their turf.

- I would rather watch the food network than MTV.

- Whenever I put on a set of chef whites, I beam with pride.

- I will try any new food that is placed in front of me.

- I can work with just about anybody.

- I get great joy from cooking for others and watching their reactions to my food.

If you checked off seven or more of the questions, then you deserve to give cooking for a career a chance. Less than seven, start looking for something else.

In many other countries, young people are assessed early on and recommendations are made regarding the career(s) that they are best suited for. Is this lack of choice contrary to the American Way? Yes, but it might just have some merit. Remember I wanted to be a rock star or a racecar driver, fortunately, I took another path. Maybe that manager who drilled me through a three-hour interview only to deny me the opportunity for a management job until I worked my way through the kitchen was smarter than I thought.

How come the chicken isn't getting brown? Well, maybe because the person in control did not have the right aptitude or attitude to follow the necessary steps towards successful completion of the task.

Who is this Chef Person and Why am I Trying so Hard to Please Him or Her?

What is most interesting about chefs is their need to be recognized. The restaurant becomes a vehicle for building self-esteem and for making a personal statement about oneself. The end result is most often a better experience for the customer. In those operations where opportunities do not exist for this form of gratification, the product becomes industrial and the experience uneventful or stale, at best.

Now this seems like a massive generalization, but I have found, through personal trial and error, that it holds a high level of credibility. This being said, to what extent should a restaurant play into this inherent need for "self" in the operation of a foodservice?

Individuals who choose to invest two to four years of their time and thousands of dollars in tuition and supplies are certainly seeking more from a place of employment than a paycheck. From their perspective, searching for the right employer will include identifying opportunities for entrepreneurial expression even without entrepreneurial financial involvement in the business. The need to put their signature on the operation's menu, wine list, and ambience will be crucial in attracting these frustrated artists and keeping them a part of the owner's team.

This need is evident in many of the physical/visual components of the job. In recent years there has been enormous concentration on the chef's uniform, the brand of tools they use, the organizations they belong to, the recognitions they receive from their peers, their visibility in local and national media, the inclusion of their names and biographies on menus, etc. Chefs want to be loved, respected, honored, copied, and (intangibly) rewarded for their expertise and efforts. Is this wrong? In essence, the chef is a leader of the team, and like all successful leaders they carry more weight in their position if they have that swagger of confidence that others view as indicative of knowledge and that still others want to emulate.

If a restaurant wants to attract the best up-and-coming cooks, the most dynamic servers, the most loyal customers, it behooves owners to pay attention to the personal needs of the chef. Like any other artist, chefs are somewhat (personally) insecure. They need reassurance from others that they are good at what they do. Very few artists refuse to sign their work, because they need to wave their personal brand. This is the way it is.

In my hundreds of restaurant experiences as a chef and a customer, I have never had a great meal at a property that did not allow the chef to express himself/herself and sign their art, *never*. This is not to say that every operation that provided this opportunity also provided great restaurant experiences. It can backfire if the chef has nothing to back-up his/her swagger.

The successful restaurant owner needs to allow the chef to feel proprietorship for the operation. The owner must also insist that he/she spend time with the guests, spend time giving back to his/her staff, spend time as a community leader, spend time with public relations associated with the property, etc.; this is part of the job.

Obviously, there are many tasks that fall under the job description of the chef. Cost controls, hiring, training, recipe development, setting purchasing standards, and establishing production schedules are all part of a chef's daily tasks; however, the top line drives the bottom line. Unless the chef contributes to efforts that yield an increase in sales, all other tasks lose much of their importance.

It is certainly true that many of the chain restaurant operations which are quite successful do not place much, if any attention on the intangible needs of a chef's ego. It is also true that these operations fulfill a significant need in our society and do so through the provision of consistently good food and predictably efficient service. I challenge, however, anyone to state that this type of operation produces a truly memorable experience. I would also challenge any private restaurant to demonstrate long-term success when competing with the wide array of chain restaurants unless they can provide memorable experiences. UNIQUE, ENTREPRENEURIAL, SERVICE-ORIENTED, INNOVATIVE, DYNAMIC, AND, YES, SOMEWHAT EGOTISTICAL STAFF MEMBERS CREATE MEMORABLE EXPERIENCES!

As an educator I can categorize typical culinary school applicants as follows:

- Passionate, self-motivated, food artists who have eventual ownership on their minds

- Somewhat seasoned culinary pirates with a few years of experience, a reasonably high level of self-confidence, and a realization that a college education is the key to their future advancement in the field

- Home cook enthusiasts who are glued to the Food Network, know the "star chefs" by name, have numerous kitchen gadgets at home, and who love to cook for friends or family

- Window shoppers who are looking for an exciting career change that will take them away from the drudgery of their current jobs

- High school graduates who feel that college is a necessary evil, so why not pick something that will only require them to work with their hands (so they think) and will always help them to fill their stomachs

There are some things that can be taught, there are some things that can be assimilated, there are some things that can be learned through a series of mistakes, and then there is attitude. Attitude is the key to success in any chosen field. Regardless of the initial reason a student chooses to pursue a culinary education, if their attitude is positive, then the end result will be some level of success.

Time and time again, company recruiters assess their decision to hire a particular student on the student's positive outlook and willingness to learn how things are done at their particular property. Unique, entrepreneurial, service-oriented, innovative, dynamic and yes-somewhat egotistical students will more often than not wind up successful. They may stumble and even fall, they may rub some people the wrong way and even piss off the instructor and their boss, but eventually they will not only come around, but also actually add something special to the college or property that gives them a chance.

Rule of thumb: *As Guy Kawasaki, author of Rules for Revolutionaries, might say: these are the misfits, the antagonists, the pain in your butt people who will eventually rule the world, implement positive change, and make a business all that it can be.*

Any restaurant that has a desire to attract loyal, enthusiastic patrons needs to give serious thought to hiring the misfits, the frustrated culinary artists, the wannabe actor/servers, the leaders of tomorrow. These individuals will become that differentiated product that every restaurant seeks.

Think about these examples:

Individual	Restaurant	Character
Charlie Trotter	Trotter's in Chicago	Over the top, detail oriented, entrepreneurial, frustrated artist and perfectionist.
Gray Kunz	Café Gray in NYC	Over the top, detail oriented, entrepreneurial, frustrated artist and perfectionist.

Individual	Restaurant	Character
Daniel Bolud	Restaurant Daniel in NYC	Over the top, detail oriented, entrepreneurial, frustrated artist and perfectionist.
David Burke	David Burke and Donatello in NYC	Intense, innovative, entrepreneurial, frustrated artist and perfectionist.
Bradley Ogden	Bradley Ogden in Las Vegas	Intense, passionate, entrepreneurial, frustrated artist and perfectionist.
Lidia Bastianich	Felidia in NYC	Passionate, totally dedicated, entrepreneurial, frustrated artist and perfectionist.
Mario Batali	Babbo in NYC	Intense, high-energy, innovative, passionate, entrepreneurial, frustrated artist and perfectionist.
Thomas Keller	The French Laundry in Yountville and Per Se in NYC	Intense, totally dedicated, entrepreneurial, frustrated artist and perfectionist.
Marc Meneau	L'Esperance in Vezelay, France	Intense, dedicated, passionate, frustrated artist and perfectionist.

The list could go on and on, but I think you get the point. Each of these individuals is the proud owner of a sizeable ego. They can, however, back it up with real skills, incredible knowledge, intense dedication, and true entrepreneurial spirit. Can you imagine any of their restaurants succeeding without their presence? People (guests) are looking for restaurant relationships, not simply a place to fill their stomachs. There are tens of thousands of competent operations that can successfully satisfy a customer's basic physiological needs, but the great restaurants, the ones that create memorable experiences, are always under the tutelage of a frustrated artist and perfectionist.

Serving hot food hot and cold food cold, serving from the left and clearing from the right, following the "act of wine service process" are all job skills that can be taught to any reasonably intelligent individual. Great service always comes from a frustrated actor or entertainer who sees the job of service as a privilege and a foray into a career in making people happy.

Great restaurants understand this and hire accordingly. Great restaurants are patient with individuals who have some of the quirky habits and needs that go along with potential greatness, and competent culinary instructors are able to see this in budding young students, nurture it, and help the right student learn how to use this gift to better their career and the success of the employers who will eventually hire them.

France:

A real education should include exposure to other cultures. A culinary education without a true understanding of France, its history and the impact that its people have had on cuisine, would surely be lacking. It was a commitment to this belief that led me to develop a program for students in the culinary capital of the world.

I love to travel. What is amazing is how the world only becomes real when you are able to experience it live. I can remember the first time that I ever flew on a plane. It was en route to basic training at Fort Jackson, South Carolina. This trip was a great combination: a white-knuckle airplane ride with hell as the destination.

Today, putting aside recent terrorist threats, getting on a plane is a great adventure, with the wonders of the world as the destination. Think about how small the world seems in the 21st century. Any destination is possible and this current generation can safely look at time in another country as a rite of passage rather than a real luxury reserved for an elite few.

My first time in France was incredibly exciting. France, the origin of classical cooking, the source of some of the finest wines in the world, the Mecca for lovers of cheese, the home to truffles, French Escargot, foie gras, the figs of Provence, the herbs and flowers of the Mediterranean, and a deep culture of religion, art, music, and architecture.

Sharon and I arrived in France with my boss, the Academic Vice President, and her son. Parking ourselves in Paris we quickly worked our way to the Eiffel Tower. Now, keep in mind that this magnificent structure was not real. It was only something that I had read about, seen in magazines, and watched on some of the classic movies like the original Sabrina with Audrey Hepburn. To see the Eiffel Tower and touch it is something totally different. Pictures, movies and books cannot do it justice. It is awe-inspiring. To think that it was built at a time when modern cranes and construction technology did not exist is even more mind-boggling. To state that it is one of the modern wonders of the world is totally justified.

The French apparently hated the structure when it was first built. Today it is the most recognized symbol of this wonderful country and their history. From nearly any vantage point in Paris, the Eiffel Tower is a guiding light. In the evening it becomes a different structure, a beacon of hope and a reminder of what brought this country through two world wars and left it a foundation of culture throughout the world.

We rented a car and quickly moved on to Entrains sur Nohain, the sister city to Saranac Lake, our home in the States. The sister city (twinning) relationship was established by Jack Weissberg, his son Kenneth, and Saranac Lake's mayor, Bill Madden, Jr. The intent was to create a cross Atlantic exchange of ideas, art, music and people.

Jack was a part of the local flavor in Saranac Lake. He operated a bakery in the shadows of those he had experienced as an art trader in France for many years. His son, Kenneth, was both French and American. He called Paris, Nice, Entrains sur Nohain, and Saranac his homes. Kenneth speaks fluent French and English, is an international lawyer, and a brilliant repository of knowledge, particularly about history.

Entrains was home to a relative of Kenneth's. He owned a house with rolling lawns, beautiful rose gardens, and a courtyard with clinging ivy working its way up three stories of stone walls. In closing out his relative's estate, Kenneth and his wife Noelle finally decided to purchase this precious home as a respite from Parisian life during the summer and fall months.

Having been introduced to Paul Smith's College, Kenneth was convinced that the presence of a culinary school in Entrains would help to revitalize this sleepy farm town that dates back to days of Roman occupation. Our visit was designed to evaluate how this relationship could materialize.

Sometimes we avoid getting to know people until we are thrown together. On this trip, I would become friends with and an admirer of my boss, Pat, the Academic Vice President for Paul Smith's. We spent nearly two weeks together, exploring a country that was truly foreign to us, meeting people who would later become great friends, investigating opportunities that would move Paul Smith's in a new direction, and creating a truly magnificent opportunity for our students.

We arrived in central Burgundy, in close proximity to Entrains sur Nohain. Everywhere you looked were farms with sunflowers in full bloom, vineyards with ripened grapes and a peace and tranquility that is hard to find in the United States. Aside from the language barrier in the country, the people were extremely friendly and accommodating. Our French was so bad that they either had no clue what we were saying or they simply smiled at how ridiculous we sounded. We finally managed to find Entrains.

Unlike Paris, this was the real France. Burgundy is the center of culinary tradition in France and the largest wine-producing region within the country's borders. We were in for a treat.

Pat had really done her homework before the trip, and while driving the three-plus hours to Entrains, she proceeded to educate all of us. One particular lesson focused on protocol and etiquette. As an example, she referred to how the French are greeted, how they approach their daily routine, and even how they attend to various rooms in their homes. Examples included, French women do not like people to come into their kitchen during the preparation of a meal and bathroom doors always remain closed, even when they are unoccupied. She said this with a certain amount of confidence.

Knocking at the door of the Weisberg's home, we were greeted by Noelle, Kenneth's wife. Immediately, we felt at home. This would be the beginning of a very important business relationship, but more importantly, a strong friendship.

Of course, as would be the case numerous times in the future, Kenneth had larger plans at that time than the College was prepared for. His idea was to have the college purchase a chateau on the edge of Entrains and convert it into an American culinary school in France. He truly believed this would be beneficial for both Paul Smith's and the town of Entrains. The College was in no position to make such a purchase so our initial visit focused on building friendships in the community and touring the area, envisioning other opportunities for the present.

During our first visit, we stayed in the oldest and possibly most sophisticated home in town. Our host, Mssr. Carre' was an aristocrat farmer who now lived by himself. He seemed very nice. Our first morning there we woke at around 7 a.m. And found our way down to the kitchen for breakfast. Mssr. Carre' was already gone, plowing the back forty. He had graciously set out breakfast for us. Baguette, confiture (jams and jellies), croissant, pain au chocolat, and coffee greeted us at the Carre' table. On the table were rather large bowls, which we assumed were for cereal. This is, after all, what everyone eats for breakfast. We searched high and low for cereal and coffee cups. Neither could be found. Later we would discover that the bowls were for Cafe' au Lait (coffee with scalded milk), and that cereal is strictly an American obsession.

We toured, tasted, networked and drank wine all day. Arriving back at Mssr. Carre's home around 9 p.m. we were ready to call it a day. Asleep and comfortable, we were startled awake at two or three a.m. by Mssr. Carre', who was very drunk, pounding on our doors and shouting in French. We locked our room doors and waited for him to tire.

The next morning, apparently the farmer's day off, I walked out of our room at around eight in search of that wonderful coffee. Now, remember Pat's lecture on French protocol and her insistence that bathroom doors always remain closed? Well, apparently they only need to be closed when unoccupied. As I walked down the hall, Mssr. Carre', stark naked and standing by the bathroom sink, simply said "Bon jour!"

The Chateau Flacy (the property that Kenneth thought we should purchase) was currently used as a home for foster children and a summer site for a musician's camp. Young classical musicians from central France would converge on Chateau Flacy for a few weeks of intense practice and training with professional cellists, violinists, pianists and woodwind artists. The Chateau was alive with music.

The culmination was a music festival that stretched through the region and featured professionals and students. This would eventually spread to Saranac Lake, as exchanges of artists and spectators made the trek to both sides of the Atlantic.

A few days into our visit, Kenneth informed me that it would be wise for us to present a unifying meal for these young artists at the Chateau Flacy. It would demonstrate respect and help to bridge the distance between our two countries. Kenneth would also invite the Duke and Duchess from the region as our guests of honor. I agreed, under the premise that the cooks from Flacy and some local cooks would join forces in presenting a dinner to approximately 60 musicians and dignitaries.

I wanted to plan a typical Burgundian meal and demonstrate to the French that an American can cook like a Frenchman. I chose coq au vin as the main course and to add a bit of Americana, Sharon (a terrific baker) volunteered to make traditional strawberry shortcake.

This was a simple meal I had prepared many times and a dessert that Sharon had made at home multiple times each year. The problems, however, were numerous. I ordered young chickens for the coq au vin, only to be informed by Kenneth that coq au vin is classically made with rooster. I changed it to chicken in wine. The chickens arrived, complete with head, feet and pinfeathers.

I had to pluck and burn off the feathers and quills and deal respectively with the head and feet. This, of course, added substantial time to preparation. The local help and assistance from the cooks of Flacy was misinterpreted. The cooks saw it as a day off and the local talent did not exist. My help in the kitchen turned out to be Paul Smith's Academic Vice President's teenage son, Phil, who had never worked in a kitchen, and Sharon as the pastry chef. This would become a turning point in Phil's life. For some reason he decided that he wanted to become a chef and enrolled in Paul Smith's culinary program immediately after high school graduation.

The strawberry shortcake became a problem, since strawberries were unavailable, the flour in France turned out to be quite different in its gluten content, and all measuring devices and oven calibrations were metric. The result was that all-American classic—fresh apricot shortcake with crème fraiche.

Kenneth kept inviting people after the supplies were in and production had begun. He simply felt that we could just cut everything smaller if necessary.

My boss, the Academic Vice President, agreed to coordinate the front-of-the-house. As a chemistry teacher, she was certainly qualified. Her staff was the foster children from Flacy and her biggest challenge was that they spoke only French and she spoke only English. Her methodology was classic, she simply talked slower and louder. At one point, approximately 30 minutes before the guests were to arrive, and a stressed out chemistry teacher/dining room manager approached me and asked: "WHAT. TIME.. ARE.. YOU.. PLANNING.. ON.. SERVING..?" This was offered very slowly and loudly. My response that allowed us both to break the tension and laugh for quite some time, was; "Pat, I speak English".

Well, we got through the meal, to rave reviews, and our diplomatic ties with Entrains were firmly established.

France is a remarkable country. Agriculturally, the commitment to grapes is unsurpassed. Throughout Burgundy and Bordeaux, there are grape vines as far as you can see. The vine of the grape resembles a tree trunk that has been twisted and tied into knots. It has been said that the trauma of the vine is directly related to the quality of the grape. The history of the grape and the wonderful fermented beverage that it produces is legendary.

After touring vineyards, chateaus, castles, museums, churches, the offices of local politicians, and individual's homes, we returned to the States with a great appreciation for the French and a list of ideas on how to proceed.

In 1993, Paul Smith's sent its first students abroad. New programs are difficult to get off the ground. When you add the complexity of international regulations and the transition to another culture, this difficulty is compounded. Through the efforts of Kenneth and Noelle Weissberg, arrangements were made for a short visit to Paris, a cluster of cultural tours through the Burgundy region, housing and meals at the Chateau Flacy in Entrains sur Nohain, and permission for our students to work in restaurant kitchens. Initially, only four students would participate on an externship abroad. The revenue barely covered the costs associated with the venture, but we were able to break the ice and formulate a program for the future.

I applaud the four daring souls who took the risk of involvement in a program that was still being developed. Overall, the experience was wonderful, but there were numerous challenges for both the students and the faculty member who was responsible for the program.

The Chateau Flacy was probably haunted. It certainly fit the bill as a large, stone, turn-of-the-century building with massive staircases, numerous nooks and crannies, and a kitchen in the caverns of the first floor and basement. Our students were placed in two renovated suites on the fourth floor of the chateau. A separate internal staircase connected the main portion of the building to this isolated wing. Jean-Louis, the local doctor and mentor of the foster child program at Flacy, had made some very nice accommodations for our students, including an American style bathroom, comfortable furniture, and even a large screen television with satellite dish connection.

At times throughout this first summer, our students were the only four people in the Chateau, perpetuating the feelings of the haunted house.

The food was, let's say; unique for American palates. This was the French version of institutional food prepared by very nice, but less than professionally trained cooks. This was fine, since Kenneth and Noelle filled in the gaps and students were able to eat at the properties where they worked.

The people of Entrains are wonderful, but again, first impressions can be deceiving. When you first arrive in Entrains it looks like a ghost town. Since most homes have a courtyard, this is where family activity takes place. Unlike America where people cluster on the streets, in Entrains the streets are bare except when roving markets come to town.

Some interesting points include the presence of three boulangeries and a patisserie in a town of around 1,200 residents. The French do love their bread. Entrains is also connected by tunnels that were used at various times in history when the town was under siege. This was a way for inhabitants to either hide or escape. Today, many of these tunnels have become the personal wine caves of families who own the homes.

Work was very different. The uniqueness of having Americans in their kitchens was amusing to the participating chefs. Most were very accommodating, considering the language barrier. Since two of the four students were women, the challenges were even greater, since women did not traditionally work in formal French kitchens. One student, Amanda, worked at a small, wonderful restaurant in a town called Varzy. The chef is excellent and has a superb reputation in the region. He was not comfortable with a woman in the kitchen, and although he treated her well, he would not allow her to complete any important culinary tasks. The other woman, Danielle, wound up at Marc Meneau's three-star L'Esperance restaurant in Vezelay. This is a world-renowned property that received strong accolades from the Michelin Guide. Chef Meneau ran a tight ship, with more than 20 cooks in his kitchen at any given time. Danielle was the first woman ever to work in his kitchen. She was well received and was quickly assigned to line work, even though she could not speak French.

My first visit to L'Esperance included one of the most memorable dining experiences of my life. The property is classic country French with manicured gardens and walking paths so that diners can stretch between courses. The kitchen was true Escoffier brigade, organized, professional and absolutely spotless. Everything was prepared a la' minute (when it is ordered), thus traditional mise en place with pots of sauces in bain maries, pre-fabricated fish, sliced mushrooms and minced pot herbs, did not exist at Meneau's. When it was ordered, it was prepared.

Apparently, since L'Esperance was the proud recipient of three Michelin stars at the time, people would fly from all corners of the world into the closest airport and shuttle to the restaurant for lunch or dinner.

With seven other guests, we experienced lunch at Meneau's tribute to Haute Cuisine. The two most memorable parts of the menu were the first two courses. Meneau would begin the dining experience with a cromique, which is a trademark amuse' at L'Esperance. pate du foie gras with truffle and cognac is set-up in raviers to a thickness of approximately one inch. The following day it is cut in cubes and over a couple days is lightly dredged in seasoned flour. The cromique is deep fried just before service and presented with tongs to each diner. You are instructed to place the foie gras in your mouth and close your lips, allowing the cromique to melt in your mouth.

It is so incredibly rich and delicious, so aromatic, so silky smooth, so extraordinarily good that you feel it in your sinus cavities, in your nose, on your tongue and masking all of your taste buds, sliding down your throat and gently settling into a groove throughout your digestive system. It is simply stated, the most sensual food I have ever eaten. You want a basket of these suckers for your meal, but the place is too proper for any diner to make a scene by demanding more.

The second course was turbot that was seasoned and fried. All of the turbot, including the bones, were fried and edible. The presentation was superb, yet simple and the flavors, including the gentle crunch of the bones, stimulated all of the senses. This was dining, not eating. Finally, the difference was clear.

Wine tastings, tours of chateaus, shopping for cheese, visits to castles and basilicas, strolls through museums and interesting work in restaurants where every thing done is serious business. This experience would likely change the lives of the four initial student participants and open the doors for improvements and expansions to this dynamic semester abroad for Paul Smith's and its students.

The program grew over the years, changing from an externship to an internship, adding courses to the program and a one-week stint at Le Cordon Bleu in Paris. By 2002, more than 130 students had completed a semester abroad as part of their culinary or hotel management degree.

Three years later, the program changed from an externship to an internship. This required significant changes to the scope of the program, including the addition of classes to the program, modifications to the cultural experience in Paris with inclusion of five days at Le Cordon Bleu, language lessons, and a travel week that allowed students to plan an educational trip at the end of the work program.

Students could choose to participate in either a summer or fall program. If they chose the summer, there was a greater emphasis on restaurant work, and if they chose the fall, they worked the vendage, or harvest of the grape, at one of many quality vineyards in the region. One such vineyard was in Sancerre, where an extraordinary Sauvignon Blanc was produced and a limited, but excellent, Pinot Noir. The vintner was Daniel Chotard, an enthusiastic, happy, but serious wine maker who relished the idea of working with our students. Since Chotard's production was small in comparison to many, our students could be involved in all aspects of wine production. They worked in the fields, pressing of the grape, and bottling.

Over the years, numerous faculty members would participate in the French program as mentors for students in the program. The first was Michael, a talented chef and teacher with an uncanny ability to acquire a working knowledge of language. At first, I think he only demonstrated an ability to sound French, but eventually was able to communicate effectively with chefs and vintners at various properties.

Then there was John, who truly loved the whole concept of European artisan bread. After a few times in France he was so enamored by the process, he built an outdoor wood-fired oven at his house to take full advantage of the well-aged starters he had been nurturing like a member of his family.

Curtiss was like a sponge. His enthusiasm for all that was French was only dampened by his dismay at how some students did not take full advantage of the opportunities to learn from the French people.

The real champion of France and the French program was Joel. Joel is my go-to guy. He has the ability to make things work, particularly when a program is either just beginning or experiencing some challenges. Just like at the Tennis Open, Joel was the one that could find the most efficient way to get things done. Over the years, he has put more than 100,000 miles of personal travel into the French Program.

Working with students in the vineyards, Joel was best at describing the experience. "When we were picking grapes, I'd take a Motrin at the beginning of a row of grapes, and take another at the end of the same row." Keep in mind that to pick the grapes, you are bent at the waist; walking up a hill at 20–30 degrees, cutting bunches of grapes and sometimes your hands at the same time. By the end of the day, hands were swollen, knees were scraped, backs were throbbing, and everyone was thoroughly sunburned.

After 10–12 hours of harvesting each day, everyone would sit around a table in Chotards home, eating wonderfully Provencal food prepared by his mother and wife, breaking off pieces of that famous French bread, and toasting many glasses of Chotard's Sauvignon Blanc.

One year, a student returned from France with incredible memories of his time with Chotard. He told me that he had personally filled and corked 14,000 bottles of the previous years Chotard vintage. That was every bottle for that year. No matter where that wine turned up, if it was a 1997 vintage, he had made his mark in preparing it for market.

In 2001, Daniel Choutard and his wife traveled to the United States and Paul Smith's to talk to our students about wine making and allow them to taste the fruits of his labor. Although he spoke very little English, his message came through very clear.

On a subsequent visit to France, Sharon and I flew into Nice to meet the Weissbergs. I had visited central Burgundy and Paris several times and was looking forward to seeing how we could incorporate Provence and the Mediterranean into the program.

Nice is magnificent, and very different from Burgundy. Flying into the airport at Nice, you approach by circling over the aqua marine color of the Mediterranean Sea and landing on a runway that begins at the water's edge.

The town has more of an Italian and Greek feel to it, with terra cotta roof tiles and white stucco building exteriors. This was definitely more of a tourist spot, with hotels and restaurants lined up along the coastline, and beautiful white sand beaches as far as you could see.

I had two missions while in Nice. First was to look at ways to incorporate this coastal, simpler cuisine into the internship program, and second to visit the home of Escoffier in Ville neuf Lobert, just a short distance from Nice.

The cuisine is honest. Simple ingredients, very fresh, without the pretension of the typical heavy French sauce work and complex flavors. The markets were dazzling. Superb produce, fresh herbs, fish markets, olives, olive oil, superb cheeses and wonderful charcuterie. Not typically known for their wines, Provence still provides light, inexpensive and delicious wines that do not overpower the cuisine with their complexity.

Sharon and I, with the Weissbergs, toured along the Mediterranean coast driving through Cannes, Nice, and eventually to Monaco and the city of Monte Carlo. Monte Carlo is a bit surreal. It is almost too perfect, very Disneylandish. Every detail is in place, including the landscaping and the polish of brass. Even the sky seems to fit into the theme of perfection.

Unfortunately, Monte Carlo is perfectly designed for a particular audience. If you're not of the elite group of wealthy world travelers who frequent the magnificent hotels, superb restaurants and exclusive casinos that create the picture of Monte Carlo, then this place is not for you.

The setting of Monaco is perfect. Tucked into the side of cliffs along the Mediterranean, this very small country is reminiscent of a postcard picture from early James Bond movies with Sean Connery and Roger Moore.

Some nearby towns were striking in their charm. St. Paul du Vance, in particular with its cobblestone roads and walkways, rising and winding foot paths, magnificent vistas over the Provence landscape, artists and unique shops, bistros and sidewalk food vendors was so welcoming. I enjoy a magnificent soup called pistou, which was a hearty combination of indigenous fresh vegetables, substantial amounts of fresh basil, wonderful regional olive oil and fresh parmigiana cheese. The soup was served in a small storefront restaurant in St. Paul du Vance with no more than 16 seats. The owner, chef and server was the same man who was able to juggle all of these tasks and still find time to pull up a chair and talk with all of his guests. Magnificent!

The Weissberg's, as I would discover, lived in Ville neuf Lobert, early in their relationship. Before they became totally consumed by cuisine and the wines of France, they had lived a few short blocks from the home of Escoffier. Kenneth had made an appointment for us to visit the home, now museum of the greatest chef of all time.

There are things in your life that clearly represent occasions where emotions run their course, but usually not in association with cooking. This was the exception to the rule. The museum is filled with menus and manuscripts from Escoffier's life as a cook and chef, tools of the kitchen, awards and other recognitions, and on the second floor of the museum, Escoffier's desk. I walked over the desk and placed my hand on it for divine inspiration. I think I actually felt the connection.

At the end of our tour, I met the curator of the museum and the director of the Escoffier Foundation. Both spoke admirable English, so communication was not too difficult. As it turned out, they were sponsoring a world symposium on culinary education in Ville neuf Loubert in December of that year. They invited me to make a presentation on the American approach towards training tomorrow's culinarians. I was honored and shocked to be given such an opportunity.

Kenneth Weissberg agreed to assist me as an interpreter, and my name was placed on the agenda. I returned with Dave, a very talented chef and fellow instructor from Paul Smith's, to Ville neuf Loubert for the presentation that December.

The audience was rather small, but the presenters represented various countries such as France, England, Ireland, Germany, and South America. On the stage, preparing for my presentation, I was seated next to Escoffier's grandson. What an honor. Later my presentation would be published in a journal distributed by the Foundation Escoffier. *Mission accomplished.*

6

What About the Students?

Sabine, Graham, Steve, Jerome, Meredith and Jacob all found themselves registering for classes in the Culinary Arts Program of Paul Smith's College in the fall of 1987. At the moment they were totally unaware of each other, they were only focused on their chosen career track and on trying to "fit-in" at college.

All had varying levels of experience and unlike many students who start a culinary education, were certain that this was their life calling. Unfortunately, many students select culinary arts without giving the decision extensive thought and without ample research. "It sounds like fun" is a long way from the realities of a life as a cook, chef and/or restaurateur. This was not a problem for Sabine, Graham, Steve, Jerome, Meredith or Jacob. They were serious.

Ironically, serious students are often the most challenging to faculty in the first year. The simple reason lies in habits and perceptions. Cooking is a serious trade that must stem from a clear understanding of the foundations. Students with previous experience have often already developed habits and perceptions about cooking that may be a bit off center. These students can either become frustrated with taking a few steps backward or confrontational by clearly stating their understanding of a process from experience. The classroom provides learning experiences for both students and culinary faculty and the "I know better" attitude that can be portrayed is just as difficult for stubborn faculty as it is for "experienced" students.

In the first semester of intro cooking classes Steve and Jacob were chomping at the bit for more volume production; in first semester baking classes, Meredith could crank out two buttercream roses for every one that the instructor did; Sabine was irritated that too many young male students felt that they could already cook better than she, even though her background was far superior to theirs; and Graham was constantly asking when they would be able to learn more about culinary competitions. "Crawl before you walk, walk before you run," this answer never seemed to satisfy these six future stars.

Anyway, after just a few weeks of classes our six "experienced cooks" found each other and became instant friends. The common denominator was the "school of hard knocks" that they went through, but which others seemed to circumvent.

The crew studied together, ate wonderful cafeteria food together, spent time in class together and even found some time to play together. Friends for life, this is what everyone, in their hearts craves for. College is a perfect environment for that to happen as it had with our "Reality Crew."

More Friends for Life:

What I enjoy most about the culinary profession are the people. Cooks, Chefs and restaurateurs are kind members of a very large family. Now you may site some instances of vulgar language, flaring tempers, inappropriate behavior and say, "not from my experience," but believe me, once you become part of the family you will be viewed as a friend for life.

Try this on for size: The next time you visit a restaurant, any restaurant, mention to the server that you are in the food industry (student, cook, server, bartender, whatever) and ask if you could either meet the chef or see the kitchen. Guaranteed, you will receive one or more of the following: extra free courses, a glass of wine, a dessert, a visit at your table from the chef, a grand cooks tour, etc. In any case, a simple notification that you are part of the club will open immediate doors to their hearts and souls and an open invitation to join their band of friends. This works anywhere and everywhere.

I have never been to a restaurant where this did not work. Never! I have seen every kitchen that I wanted to see, met every chef that I wanted to meet, received copies of menus from nearly every restaurant that I have visited (even ones where I did not stay and eat), and collected more business cards than you can shake a stick at.

While we are on business cards: my book of friends is a three-ring binder with hundreds of business cards. Even people who I briefly met only once are considered part of this friendship bank. I feel perfectly comfortable calling them and asking for advice or an occasional favor, and many have done the same with me. Welcome to the club!

Why does this work? The answer is simple: those who have endured the pressures, those who have made the commitment, those who understand what the commitment is, those who have dedicated a good portion of their lives to food, can be fully appreciated only by those who have endured the same. Chefs are receiving more recognition today than ever before, yet 99% of the non-chef population has no idea what it really takes to operate a kitchen or run a successful restaurant. Only members of the club can truly know. It is very much like the Marines: "The few, the proud, the cooks and chefs of America".

I spent 10 hours one day in July at Alphonse Mellot's chateau in Sancerre, France. After consuming far too much wine in his private cellar, we shook hands, hugged and proclaimed each other "friends for life." *We meant it.*

After the Culinary Olympics in Frankfurt, after the trials and tribulations of two years in preparation, ten chefs and their managers and advisors were friends for life. I make it a point to talk to nearly every one of these culinary brothers every year. We are never afraid to ask each other for advice or favors, but more importantly, we are always anxious to share what is happening in our personal and professional lives. Each one is like a brother to me. What is the common bond? Food and the kitchen brought us together and keep us bound together, just like family.

Every student, every chef that I have met, every restaurateur, every food salesman (that I could tolerate), every vintner, maitre'd, sommelier, waiter, bartender, dish washer, author, and restaurant equipment manufacturer, is a friend of mine. I respect them and have a continuous interest in what they are doing. How many people outside of this crazy business can say that their network of friends is in the hundreds or even thousands. I can.

Think about it, every time a food person goes out to dinner they are not only enjoying the food, they are enjoying the company of friends who make the restaurant work.

7

A Day in the Life of Culinary School

Our "Reality Crew," despite their cynicism about starting their education with knife skills and thickening agents, were very serious students. Although they would rarely admit it to each other, there was a definite competitiveness among them. Yes, they worked and studied together and would always cheer each other on; however, if one received a better grade or a higher accolade from a chef, the rest of the crew would simply work harder to be the next one to receive praise. This attitude was never malicious (although this does happen in college environments quite often). It was, in fact, rather productive. The six stars were always at the top of their class, leaders that other students looked up to.

Unlike many of their peers, this competitiveness led the group to discovering the library, a stronghold of excellent books on culinary history, unique recipes, and restaurant management. While some had a difficult time separating the chance to party from the need to study, our six-crew members found ways to supplement what they learned in the classroom. This does not imply that they did not find ways to play; they simply learned how to prioritize when they had to.

A typical day started with alarms going off at 5 a.m. (Lab courses begin at 6 a.m.). The six had a pact that prepared for inevitable over-sleeping. All for one, one for all—the six musketeers made sure that each was awake and ready to perform in the kitchen.

Breakfast didn't always happen, but the chefs in kitchens always had coffee on and usually students could find something to eat that would keep sugar levels where they should be. Jerome found out that if he got to the lab early enough to help a chef prepare for lab, there was even an opportunity to fry a couple eggs for breakfast. It sure beat walking to the cafeteria.

Lab courses always begin with a short lecture on the material to be covered, a review of recipes to be used, and an opportunity for questions and answers.

Although students are supposed to review before arriving at class, many do not. It always amazed Sabine, Steve and the others how ill prepared many of their fellow classmates were. Most students are fairly quiet at this time of the morning, but as soon as pots and pans began to clank and the aroma of sautéed onions engulfed the room, these young cooks got into a rhythm. Kitchens were usually hopping places by 7 a.m.

My schedule allows me to arrive around 7 a.m., since I stay till 5 p.m. or so. Walking from the parking lot and seeing nearly 100 students in whites, hitting their pace in the kitchen is always motivational. Although the only customers at the end of lab were the students themselves, many of the kitchens work at a pace that would lead you to believe that a bus full of patrons was about to arrive any minute.

By 8:30 students are assembling plates for the chef's critique. One of the hardest things for chefs to learn and one of the hardest things for students to accept is critique. It takes time for both to differentiate between criticism and critique, and until that happens, tempers are always on edge. "Sabine, the presentation on this sea bass is quite good, but you definitely overcooked the fillet. The vegetables are a bit too al dente, and you were heavy handed with the salt".

Sabine's heart sank. She thought, "How can the chef say that? This is just how I learned how to prepare a similar dish at the restaurant I worked at last summer. The chef there never complained. Are my skills not up to par? Or does this chef really not know enough about food himself? That's it! I'm O.K., the chef is wrong."

In reality, students need to learn four very important things:

1. *The chef is here to help you develop a palate*

2. *Critique is meant to help you to assess the details of cooking and how to constantly improve*

3. *Some parts of cooking are subjective, yet the chef, your peers, and the customer are never wrong. If they are the ones consuming your products, it is their opinion that counts.*

4. *If critique tears you apart, your career in the kitchen will be painful*

In reality, chef instructor needs to learn four very important things:

1. *Whether you are right or wrong, nobody enjoys critique*

2. *Critique is meant to help not demean. Critique without explanation on how to improve is really criticism*

3. *People are sensitive; always point out the good attributes of a student before focusing on what needs to be improved*

4. *Avoiding critique will only intensify a student's pain when someone finally tells them the truth*

"Jacob, if I ever need someone to help me prepare saltimbocca for 500, I want you by my side. But today we are focusing on perfection of one plate so you can understand how to prepare an item the way it was meant to be prepared. Since we all understand that customers eat with their eyes, you must heed the importance of presentation. This dish tastes fine, but your presentation skills are still lacking."

Jacob, shrugged off this biting critique. To demonstrate that he was upset would certainly lower his stature in the class. Isn't cooking all about serving people in a timely fashion and minimizing steps so that the property can make money? Presentation takes time and as Sorgule said in class—time is money.

At lunch that day, each of the crew talked about their lab critiques and their personal feelings about instructor inadequacies. It was Meredith that brought the conversation to point. "Did any of you ask the chef how you could make the dish better? Did any of you ask your fellow classmates what they thought of your food? Maybe, critique is a good thing if you use it as a learning tool?"

Back to class, three more courses in the afternoon before they could meet back in the library for their daily group study session. First comes Dining Room and Kitchen Management, the student's first course dealing with the management of operations. Commonly referred to as D and K, this course, although important to a student's career, is not universally taken as seriously as cooking classes. Many students are too young to understand that a chef's job requires as great deal more than cooking.

Jacob sees an opportunity to prove his theory that the concept of food presentation pales in comparison to the timely execution of a meal and the cost effectiveness of speed. He poses the question: "Chef, in the big scheme of things, isn't speed and cost efficiency much more important than wasting time on intricate presentations of food?"

One of the interesting things about being a teacher is understanding that student-teacher interactions are no different than child-parent interactions, or for that matter, employee-supervisor interaction. Playing parent against parent, supervisor against supervisor, and in this case teacher against teacher is a common practice that has no age limit.

"Ironically, Jacob, you're right and wrong at the same time. It's imperative that you all realize that from a business perspective, the most crucial task of a chef is sales. All efforts in the back-of-the-house must be geared towards two things:

- Convince the customer to buy what you want to sell

- Convince the customer to return.

Now, how this is accomplished is both a science and an art. Visual presentation of food, although somewhat time-consuming, can add perceived value to a dish. If the value is elevated in a customer's mind, then the restaurant can actually raise the selling price. This in turn reduces the cost of goods and the overall impact of the cost of labor. On the other hand, if the kitchen is so wrapped up in presentation that they cannot get the food to the guest in a timely fashion, then the impact of the presentation is lost on an impatient customer."

Jacob, once again realized that teachers have a tendency to create more questions than answers. It would be much easier if there were just right and wrong answers. These gray areas where students are expected to evaluate a situation and come to their own conclusion was very confusing. Although Jacob was not a huge fan of accounting, at least in that class there were definitive "rights and wrongs."

Jerome found this class, and others like Human Resource Management and Menu Planning to be even more fascinating than the labs. He quickly determined that his goals in life would evolve around private entrepreneurship—the American Dream: own your own business. How to convince customers to act a certain way and how to set the stage for profitability were keys to success; he knew it even in the freshman year.

The final two classes of the day were the most difficult for the crew of six. English Composition and Math of Finance. Now, they all wanted to be chefs, why in the world would they need to develop better writing and computation skills? It wasn't until many years later that all of them discovered the answer to this question. In the meantime, they did their best to stay focused on the need to complete these courses and maintain their grade point average.

Four o'clock, all were done with classes for the day; time to meet in the library for their daily review and study session. Graham was the leader this week. They had established a plan by the end of their first month in college to rotate leadership among the group each week. This gave everyone a feeling of significance and led to a more diverse discussion of opinions.

Graham began; "I found that today was very frustrating. The first month, to most of us, was rather redundant since we all felt comfortable with knife skills and an understanding of the ingredients we were working with. Now that we are actually preparing food in its final form, it seems as if those students with little to no experience are receiving as much, if not more, praise for their cooking than we are. Granted, we all took liberties in adding a personal touch to the recipes that the chef gave us, but isn't that what being a chef is all about?"

Sabine was the first to respond; "I feel the same way, but I have to admit that those who followed the recipe and the chef's instructions produced good tasting food."

After bantering back and forth, the group proposed that a private meeting with the dean in charge of their program was in order. They needed clarification and an opportunity to explain how much better prepared they were to experiment and how sticking to recipes was counter-productive to their education. Graham called my office to set-up such a meeting.

When the group arrived for their meeting on the following day they were quite surprised at how short the meeting was. I sat them down and asked one basic question: "Have you discussed your concerns with the chef instructors responsible for your labs?"

Graham's response was, "No. We felt that this was a matter for the person who could mandate a change."

I explained that if we were to properly prepare students to work effectively in any organization, we must begin by developing an understanding of protocol and effective use of the chain of command. I also commented that cooking must be structured before it can be free form. If a cook does not appreciate the need for consistency, then they will never be effective as an interpreter of preparations.

Although disappointed, the crew did discuss their concerns with individual instructors and found a welcome receptiveness on the part of the faculty. They were told to follow the procedures like everyone else, but were offered lead team positions so that less experienced students could learn about the crews' individual kitchen stories and historical perspective on preparations and presentations.

This format of assessing the day's activities and working together as a team took our reality crew through four-years of college, exciting internship and externship experiences, and a lifetime of learning that continues today.

Today, each of these team members has reached a pinnacle in their career. Steve is working for a high volume chain restaurant as a district culinary manager with twelve restaurants under his supervision.

Sabine is an executive chef in a fine dining restaurant in Albany, New York. She is constantly dazzling her patrons with innovative interpretations of culinary classics.

Graham is executive chef for a corporate guesthouse. This major corporation uses Graham's skills to help solidify business deals over a great meal. He also found the perfect position to allow time for culinary competition. As a member of the U.S. Regional Culinary Olympic Team he left his mark on the culinary world at the 2004 competition in Germany and after another grueling tryout, he has been selected as a member of the 2008 National Team.

Jerome became an entrepreneur. Although his heart is in the kitchen, his head is in the business of operating a financially successful restaurant. Since more than 66% of the restaurants that open today are closed in a year, it is a testament to his determination and abilities to still be running strong after four years.

Meredith maintains her love of the country and the mountains, but found a home for artistic expression in the pastry department of one of Las Vegas largest hotels. As Executive Pastry Chef, she supervises more than 40 bakers as they create thousands of desserts, breakfast pastries, cakes and centerpieces each day.

Jacob is chef at a major university. He determines the menus and the quality food that thousands of students consume each day. Although his food is not four-star, it is considered some of the best in the college food service scene.

Not every student who enrolls in a culinary arts program reaches the level of success that this team of friends has. Some struggle but find a niche as a contributor to the success of a food service; some use their time in college as a period of maturation. They sometimes consider their culinary training as a "fall-back" if other pursuits don't work out. Others either start with and quickly leave the profession or decide even earlier on that they are not cut out for the type of work and the demands that a professional career in cooking brings.

In all cases, we do what we can to paint the most realistic picture for current culinarians and future chefs. That is one of the most important roles of a chef instructor. Love it or leave it, is certainly an appropriate statement when it comes to a career as chef.

8

"Back in the Saddle Again"

Oh well, change is one of the only things in life that is certain. After 26 years as a teacher and program dean, it was time for a change. Philosophical differences with the college administration led to my decision to depart and return to operations. What better place to return to than the Mirror Lake Inn, the focused operation where I received my start in the Adirondacks. Since my initial time with the Inn, it had burned to the ground, been re-built in a spectacular manner, raised to the level of a AAA 4-diamond resort, and become the driving force for quality change in Lake Placid.

I think it was Anthony Bourdain who stated that those who are still cooking in their forties are rare, and those who are over fifty realize that they probably won't live much longer anyway. Here I was, returning to the kitchen at the age of fifty-five (this could be a mistake).

I guess I had some things to prove to myself: could I still handle the physical demands of the job, could I bring something new to the table after twenty-six years in education, could I build a team that would help me to reach the culinary goals set forth? Time will tell.

Well, I must tell you, some things never change. The work is still very physical, the temperatures are still high enough to slow cook those working, purveyors are still as annoying as ever, positions are still incredibly difficult to fill, tempers are still always on edge, conflicts between front and back-of-the-house still exist, food cost control is still a constant battle, some customers still look for ways to complain, on and on.

What is comforting about returning to the battlefield? The passion for cooking, the gratification of creating food for others to enjoy, the friendly banter that continues to drive conversations in the kitchen, the realization that every day is different with different challenges and opportunities is truly comforting. This is what brings a smile back to my face on most days.

Restaurant people are real. They work hard, are creative, typically jump in to make things work even when they are on the precipice of chaos, have sensitive feelings regardless of how many tattoos are on their arms, and care about others even though they might talk otherwise. They are real people, performing sometimes super-human tasks, every day of the week.

I am not sure how long I can do this, but I do know that my first year has been humbling. It has made me more intuitive, stronger as a self-assessor, far more objective, more cautious about what others think, far more guest-oriented, and if I ever returned to it—a better teacher who did it and has done it again.

Culinary schools have helped a dynamic industry become even more so, but have likely created some misconceptions on the part of those who invest heavily in becoming a chef. Here is a taste of reality:

- We have one rolling pin, about a dozen stainless bowls, one 6 quart kitchen aid mixer, ranges and ovens that have been through war—but are brought back to life a few times each year with a tune-up, never enough small utensils, sauté pans that are getting thinner by the day, and limited amounts of china (we all cringe anytime a plate is dropped). Deal with it; cost must be controlled in a business. The days of storerooms full of extra equipment (often donated by industry) in your regional cooking school are over. Make it work with what you have!

- Not every employee has a formal education in the culinary arts and might not know the difference between a small dice and a brunoise, the proper way to make a stock, how to perfectly braise a veal shank, or even how to peel a tomato. With time, they will learn, once you convince them that your way makes sense.

- Every peel of onion, every bone from fish, every leftover grain of rice costs the operation money. Profitability is very fragile and must become everyone's focus.

- Dishwashers will come and go, cooks will find better opportunities elsewhere, competitors will pirate your better line cooks, purveyors will lie and disappoint you, customers will take your heart away with one bad comment, burns and cuts are a way of life, and yes, forget about holidays. Deal with it!

I returned to the kitchen for a few very specific reasons. Yes, I was discouraged about the bureaucracy in colleges; yes, I was philosophically opposed to the vision of the last president I worked for; but more importantly I wanted to refresh and see how the industry had changed and see how well, or not so well, I could again take the helm and be successful. What is most fortunate for me is that the crew of culinarians that surround me care deeply about what they do. They sweat the small stuff, take pride in a busy night, smile when an occasional customer says "Wow," lose sleep when an occasional customer is not pleased, get pumped up when we "meet our numbers," and gladly tell people on the street where they work. This is what brings me back every day.

There were many things that I preached in my classes over the years that are absolutely true:

- Restaurants are only marginally profitable at best and live on the precipice of disaster every day.

- Labor cost is the straw that breaks the camel's back, yet it is that same labor that can bring a restaurant to greatness.

- When you need them to come through for you, many purveyors will disappoint you. Watch them closely.

- When you find a salesman and a purveyor that you can really trust, buy from them. Even if they are a bit more expensive, service and trust rule.

- Everything is everybody's job in a restaurant. If an employee ever says or implies that something, anything is not their job, start to look for a way to get rid of them.

- Your menu as a chef must be their menu as well. Press on with your philosophy and standards, but give all of your cooks a chance to put their mark on the menu.

- Joke with them, push them, bring important points home as strongly as you need to, but always thank them for their contributions. Do it daily and do it often.

- Don't embarrass your staff. If you need to make a point do it with tact and do it away from the crowd. It is not the critique that brings them down; it is the manner with which it is delivered.

- Don't allow an item to leave your kitchen that fails to meet your standards. Make sure that your cooks enforce this rule even when you are not there.

- It is all about the food, it is all about the service, and it is all about the experience. Everything counts and not one can support your operation without the others.

I am deeply proud of the food that we serve at the Mirror Lake Inn. I am personally hurt when we drop the ball and fail to exceed a customer's expectations. I, like many of my cooks, lose sleep every night thinking about what we are doing, how we are doing it, what could go wrong, how can we recover if something does go wrong, how we can improve, where we will find the best staff, how others perceive our work, etc. This is something that most customers do not realize. A serious restaurant has very serious, insecure, fragile people who live to see clean plates returning to the kitchen dish area. After all, no other art form is subject to such instantaneous critique. Career cooks don't do it for the money (the money is important, but there are many other fields that would pay more); they do because it is what they were meant to.

I take great pride in the graduates whom I had some level of impact on. Those who are still in the field and who would be classified as "serious" cooks and chefs all share the same or similar quirks that I do. This business attracts people who can easily be categorized. It is what it is, it is wonderful, it is difficult, it is rewarding and it is heartbreaking. Do you fit? That is the question.

How come the chicken isn't getting brown is a question that will be asked of chefs throughout time. Many of those who will ask at the age of 18 or 19 may grow to become the next great chefs of a generation. Before we criticize the question, look into their eyes and see if they have the heart for this business and the passion to become exceptional. If they do, smile and demonstrate how to fry chicken.

9

Joys and Tribulations of Travel and Networking:

One of the best ways for a chef to improve his or her cooking is to travel and discover what others already know. There are very few things in cooking that are truly new; however, every cook has the honor of interpreting them differently.

I suppose everyone has their list of things they have to do in a lifetime. It might be natural wonders to see, mountains to climb, cars to drive, music to hear, etc. Chefs have food to eat and restaurants to experience.

My list is long, but getting shorter all the time. The ability of a chef instructor to teach is greatly enhanced by the anecdotal kitchen experiences they can share and the meals that they have enjoyed. I have been on this mission of research and development for quite some years. These are some of those experiences.

Aquavit:

In 1995 I added a new "must experience" restaurant to my list. I heard through the grapevine about a fine dining Scandinavian restaurant in New York City. This restaurant, called Aquavit after the intense caraway-flavored vodka of Norway, Sweden and Finland, was supposedly the "real thing". Having come from Norwegian stock, it was only natural I needed to experience Scandinavian cuisine.

A reservation was made and five of us were prepared for a unique dining opportunity. The restaurant is tucked away in a beautifully appointed building on 56th street. Only a simple 18-inch plaque with "aquavit" identifies the existence of this Mecca for gourmands. No elaborate signage, no posted menu, not even a designation that this is a restaurant. For all intents and purposes it could be an exclusive brokerage or protected home of fine imported glass or porcelain.

Once inside, we were professionally greeted and ushered into the first floor lounge with large glass beakers of home flavored aquavit and simple yet elegant

Scandinavian furniture and lighting. After a few moments we were directed downstairs to the dining room with its featured black granite wall and waterfall. The room is again simple but elegant in the style of modern Scandinavian architecture.

The meal was extraordinary. Fresh Arctic char, wonderfully pickled herring and cured salmon, reindeer and caribou, superb Scandinavian cheeses and absolutely delicious Norwegian flatbread. The service was impeccable, yet not overbearing, and each course drew us away from our conversation so we could savor every bite.

As is the custom of my group of dining friends, whenever we find a new restaurant we always plan our menu orders as a group so that we have a chance to try as much of the chef's cuisine as possible. Once served, we taste and pass, taste and pass. To some this may seem unusual and even rude, but to any chef this is a great compliment.

On this occasion, I selected a double lamb consommé' with quenelles of foie gras for an appetizer. It was over the edge. Absolutely the most delicious thing I had ever tasted. While others were passing their appetizers I was protecting my as if it were gold bullion. I hoarded the consommé' myself and shrugged off the stares of discontent from my friends. This one was all mine.

The chef at Aquavit is Marcus Samuelsson. He was born in Africa, educated as an Englishman, and trained as a chef in Sweden. This variety of backgrounds helped to create a tremendously talented chef who has since taken New York by storm. In 2003, he was awarded best New York Chef by the James Beard Foundation.

Since our initial visit, I have returned many times to Aquavit and have recommended it to those people I consider my close friends. Without exception, each person that I recommended Aquavit to has called to thank me afterwards. It is as if I bestowed something special on them that changed their culinary perspective. However, I only passed on an address.

Gotham Bar and Grill:

Having grown up in Buffalo, I always keep a eye open for any successful artists, musicians, athletes, and chefs who at some point in their lives claimed Buffalo as their home. On another visit to New York in 1996, I made reservations at one of the top three busiest fine dining restaurants in the city. Gotham Bar and Grill, located in Tribeca, is now world renowned. The chef, Alfred Portale, was born in Buffalo and made his mark on New York with the introduction of 'vertical cuisine." Alfred's masterful plate designs accentuate the "wow" in food presentation. In fact, they appear to be as much a statement of architectural and engineering design as they are culinary art.

The restaurant is fun and classy at the same time. Fabric draped from the ceiling helps to add warmth to the room and dampen the noise of excited patrons. Unlike Samulesson's masterful petite portions, Portale creates height to his plates and brings an illusion of larger quantities by building lightness or "air" into his plate designs. The food is remarkable, the staff very knowledgeable, the wines appropriate to the menu, and the flavors at the top of the scale.

I have been back to Gotham many times and have even planned tasting luncheons there for small groups of students. Each time, the chef plans a special menu for the group, prints menus dedicated to Paul Smith's College and if he is in town, always visits the table and talks to the group of young culinarians.

Lutece:

There are a handful of chefs in the United States whom everyone respects, individuals who personify all that is wonderful about food and the industry that serves it and who are professional and ethical beyond reproach. Andre' Soltner is one of those chefs.

I can't remember the year, but as the New York Hotel Show was approaching I read an article stating that Andre was about to retire and sell his world-famous Lutece' Restaurant. This operation for more than 30 years had been rated one of the finest restaurants in the world and one of the two best French restaurants in America. I had to sample this chef's food before he packed up his knife kit and left.

I made a reservation for Tim (the fellow instructor referred to as the Mayor of Food Village from the U.S. Tennis Open) and our current college president. We were in!

Lutece' like Aquavit is in a semi-residential part of Manhattan and is only designated by a small brass plaque with the word, Lutece' etched on its surface. The building was once a private home converted by Soltner into this bastion of culinary excellence.

Now I need to preface the meal with a short tale about Soltner. Every serious cook knows who he is, but few have had the opportunity to meet him, simply because he never left his restaurant. *Never!* At an American Culinary Federation Convention, Chef Soltner was listed as one of the keynote speakers. I was excited to hear from this masterful technician so I registered for the convention.

Soltner spoke with a great authority and a passion for cooking that was mesmerizing. I can't remember the entire context of his presentation, but for these words: "Ladies and gentlemen, we should not get too wrapped up in all of the nonsense of being a chef. We should always remember that first and foremost, we are cooks." To an audience full of people who in their perfectly starched whites adorned with medals for this and that, no more important words could ever have been spoken.

As we were seated in Lutece' by our waiter who was surely 75 or older, I was taken aback by the warmth and hominess of the restaurant. I felt as though I were having dinner in Andre's home dining room. As is usually the case, I pass my business card to our waiter and said that if there were an appropriate time, I would love to meet the chef.

Our waiter may have been older than most; however, his complete knowledge of the food, wine and service of this meal was unsurpassed. An amuse' was delivered to the table prior to our first ordered course, and to our surprise, Soltner accompanied the course. He pulled up a chair and joined us for this introductory tidbit, asking with great interest about our school and its students. I can't remember what the amuse' was because I was so in tune with the chef's presence. To me, he represented all that a chef could be, thus my attention was on his every word.

The balance of the meal was superb, featuring simple, classical French food that was prepared to perfection. From the petite frog legs to the perfectly pan seared Muscovy duck, everything was as good as it gets.

A few months later Soltner retired and sold the restaurant. It remained open under new ownership for a period of time, but I could never return, for fear of spoiling the moment in my mind.

Montrachet:

SoHo and Tribeca are centers of creative culinary arts in New York. In the early eighties, I heard of a fairly new restaurant in Tribeca that was receiving rave reviews. Montrachet featured American interpretations of French food, with a stellar wine list to match. It would be ten more years before I actually made a reservation. I did so because one of the partners and managing owners spends a considerable amount of time at his mountain respite close to Paul Smith's. Tony Zazula frequented our celebrations and fund-raising dinners at Paul Smith's and as I became acquainted with him, our conversations always drifted towards food and wine. I made the reservation with great anticipation.

Montrachet, like Lutece', exudes a warm feeling of being in someone's home. Muted colors, crisp white tablecloths, servers in black and white and an inviting, richly appointed bar and visible wine selection make you feel immediately at home. Tony was expecting us and gave the chef license to show off. The tasting menu with accompanying wines was so exceptional that Montrachet is now my favorite New York restaurant (followed closely by Aquavit). The wine list is rated one of the best in New York, and as the sommelier states, there is nothing on the list that is less than exceptional.

Over the years I have taken small groups of special students to Montrachet as their introduction to fine dining. On one such event, a student said; "Now I know the difference between eating and dining."

Restaurant Associates:

Dining is an experience, and should be viewed as such. All the human senses are stimulated when the restaurant experience moves from eating to dining. Chefs would like to state that everything revolves around the food, but successful restaurateurs know that it is much more than that. There are few companies in the United States that are better at defining the "dining" experience than Restaurant Associates. Yes, this is the same company that served thousands of char-grilled hamburgers at the Tennis Open, but first and foremost, they have always been a "restaurant company" providing some of the most unique venues to be found.

Three examples really stand out: The "Center of the Universe" is often the label given to Rockefeller Center in New York City. The apex of this "center" is the sheet of ice at the foot of the NBC building. This is the most visible skating venue in the world, the same sheet that welcomes the world to the famous Rock Center Christmas Tree every year.

Surrounding the skating rink are three restaurants, all with spectacular front row views of the skaters. All of these are operated by Restaurant Associates. The flagship fine dining operation among them is Sea Grill. A glass and brass elevator carries guests from street level (across from the NBC Today Show studios) to the restaurant entrance, underground. The restaurant was re-designed by John Portman, a world-renowned architect who is best known for his atrium style hotels in Atlanta and New York. The concept was to maximize the view of "the ice" and take full advantage of natural and man-made light. The view is incredible.

The food certainly matches the experience, including some of the finest fresh fish in New York. It is, however, the "whole package" that makes Sea Grill a "must experience" restaurant in New York.

Other Restaurant Associate properties include Brasserie, Naples, Cafe' Centro, Cucina, Tropico and many more. The company, known for these operations, is even more exceptional when it comes to the provision of what many would call "institutional" food.

Lincoln Center, Conde Nast Headquarters the Museum of Natural History, Sony Headquarters, the United Nations, Carnegie Hall and numerous other office buildings and cultural centers in New York are home to Restaurant Associate Food Service. To call these operations, "institutional" is a disservice. The food and service are equal to the finest centers of haute cuisine in the City and truly set the benchmark for what corporate dining can and should be.

Aureole:

Charlie Palmer is a class act. Not only is his food exceptionally well prepared, but the ambience and service in this restaurant/home is unsurpassed. I took a group of students here for a tasting lunch and when the maitre'd discovered these were tomorrow's chefs and managers, he rolled out the red carpet: extra courses, dialogue about the restaurant and a tour of the kitchen.

I had an opportunity a year later to dine in Aureole in Las Vegas. The food is equally good, but the ambience is totally different. You enter high above the dining room floor and walk down a circular staircase that encases a Plexiglas cube that holds the restaurant's collection of wines. The cube is easily 30 feet high, with thousands of bottles protruding from all four sides. The most unique feature is not the Plexiglas or the wine; it is how the wine is retrieved. Attractive, young women(called wine angels) in black leotards hook a cable to their belts and are hoisted up at various levels to pick out the wines that tables order throughout the evening. I think that many people order more wine than they should consume just to watch this interesting process take place.

Charlie Trotter's:

The Trotter experience does not begin when you are first seated in this Chicago destination; it begins when you first receive confirmation of your reservation. I have had the pleasure to dine at this fabulous restaurant a number of times, but none can compare to that first experience. Our reservation was confirmed four months in advance and I quickly began to read all that I could about this culinary perfectionist. His cookbooks, articles about the operation, comments from friends who had already made the sojourn, I was determined to draw all that I could from the forthcoming dining adventure.

Some of the subtleties may have been lost on others, but when I walked through the door of this unpretentious restaurant entranceway, I began to compare my notes to the real thing. Impeccably clean, bar back bottles organized as if a librarian were in charge, greetings by name although I had never been there before, serious professionals in black and whites, and an aura of anticipation that was shared by diners and employees alike.

Throughout the evening, each course brought new taste sensations, each wine pairing was an education, every nuance of service was by the book, and it was truly remarkable. My typical transfer of business card yielded a tour of the kitchen, a meeting with Charlie Trotter, a view of their extraordinary wine cellar, and a signed menu for my collection. This was a night to remember.

In subsequent visits, the food and service were just as extraordinary culminating in two adventures at the special chef's table in the kitchen where Trotter and his cadre of professionals simply cooked for us outside the parameters of a menu. The price was close to the national debt, but the experience was priceless.

Frontera Grill/Topolobambo:

Rick Bayless is a rare chef whose roots are as much a study in Mexican history and culture as they are cooking. He speaks of the cuisine of Mexico from a knowledge that appears to be limitless. It has been said that Frontera and Topolobambo represent the most authentic Mexican food north of Mexico itself.

American palates are typically jaded with Americanized Tex/Mex food renditions, and as was the case with me, are pleasantly surprised at the depth of complexity that Bayless exhibits in his restaurants. From the incredible margaritas to the wonderful mole sauce, this is real food.

Gary Danko:

Gary Danko was born and raised in the Adirondacks of New York, so obviously when I heard of his restaurant in San Francisco, it became a destination. Whatever Trotter exhibits in culinary perfection, Danko emulates with a twist. A restaurant that is simply elegant and well positioned in the Fisherman's Wharf district of San Francisco, excels in food, wine and service and comes off as well as Charlie Trotter's, but is a bit more laid back.

Durgin Park:

On the opposite side of every restaurant previously mentioned, Durgin Park is a treasure that defies description. The portions are huge, the lines are long, the flavors are great, the menu is classic Boston, and the location in Quincy Market is ideal. What sets this landmark apart from others is the fun banter that takes place between their well-seasoned servers and the public. Some might even consider it a bit crusty or even borderline offensive, but to a restaurant person who has spent his life subservient to the guest, this is a breath of fresh air.

The endless lines of eager guests demonstrate that there is a need for this type of experience, although I doubt that others could pull it off as well.

The list goes on and on of dozens of exceptional restaurants that have become a part of me. Every time that I work with my staff to develop a menu or a new dish, I reflect back on those countless experiences that make up my repertoire. In the culinary universe there is little that does not owe a great deal to the endless experiences of cooks and chefs learning from each other, borrowing ideas, adding a twist to make it uniquely theirs, and building this data base that is part of the public domain. I cannot thank all of these chefs enough for how they have contributed to my own definition of "my cuisine."

It is the responsibility of every serious cook, chef, restaurateur and chef instructor to travel, network, share, build his or her culinary memory bank and pass on their experiences to others.

Author's Notes

✦

Living Your Life Through Others

There comes a point in your life when you realize that however fruitful your personal time has been, the most enjoyable way to live success is through other people who you have touched.

Parents realize that there is incredible satisfaction drawn from the experiences and successes of their children. In all cases, pride in their accomplishments is one of the greatest feelings you can have. In some cases, we encourage our children to pursue opportunities we had an interest in, but never fully acted on (for various reasons).

Sharon and I are incredibly proud of our three children. All are doing those things that bring them joy, all continue to grow into wonderfully kind, intelligent, and talented adults, and all of them are uniquely their own person.

Erika, from the time she was 10 or 12 years old, knew she wanted to be an artist. I have never seen a person so totally committed to excellence in any field as she is to all forms of art. Her dedication is so extreme that sometimes we find ourselves telling her to stop working or studying for a bit and go out and have fun!

Critique is something that we can all grow from, something that to varying degrees we all dread, and something that generally comes from others. Erika's greatest critic is herself. The sign of a craftsperson is their level of commitment to excellence. Hers is off the charts. Today, she is applying all of her love of art to a budding career. Working as a store visual designer in Portland, Oregon, she uses her background in graphics, painting, three dimensional design, color complementation, photography and crafts.

Watching Jessica evolve as a person is totally enjoyable. An avid runner; somewhat streetwise Montrealer; solid student of psychology, management and social issues; and assessor of human interaction, she continues to evolve into a person that she wants to be.

Jess is a person who, once set on a goal, pushes herself to reach it. Looking for a different experience than growing up in the Adirondacks, she insisted on attending college in an international city. Against my better judgment, this was the path that she took. Her decision turned out to be the right one. I was wrong. She spent a summer in Maine seeking to make sense out of her choice of management as a major and many inherent conflicts she noticed with numerous companies who did not share her awareness of social and environmental issues. It was the right decision for her. Today, she works and gives back to others through a rewarding career in Burlington, Vermont.

While both girls grew up in the Adirondacks and spent time in cities away from the woods, mountains and lakes, they wound up harboring a tremendous love for the area that they called home for 18 years before branching out. Coming home to them will always mean coming to the Adirondacks.

Our son Leif is a terrific person. Intelligent, likeable, athletic, and self-motivated, he has maintained these great qualities while suffering through the normal phase of teenage uncertainty.

Leif loves to ski more than anything else. He knows how important performance in school is and wrestled, as most teenagers did, with what path to take with a career. In the back of his mind, all success will revolve to some degree around his ability to continue to pursue skiing. It is always refreshing to see this level of dedication. Off to college now, his future will take him in a direction that involves engineering principles and technology teaching (how ironic), something he has developed a strong interest in while observing a teacher that he respects and admires.

A side benefit to becoming a teacher is that you now have hundreds or thousands of avenues to measure your success in life through others. My extended family includes nearly every student who sat in my classrooms or worked in my kitchens. Their success brings me a tremendous sense of gratification. "Sadly" their failures also bring a sense of dismay.

978-0-595-43695-8
0-595-43695-1

Printed in the United States
86134LV00012B/150/A